The Digital Project Management Evolution

The Digital Project Management Evolution

Essential Case Studies from Organisations in the Middle East

Shafiz Affendi Mohd Yusof and Kamal Jaafar

Routledge
Taylor & Francis Group

A PRODUCTIVITY PRESS BOOK

First edition published in 2020
by Routledge/Productivity Press
52 Vanderbilt Avenue, 11th Floor New York, NY 10017
2 Park Square, Milton Park, Abingdon, Oxon OX14 4RN, UK

© 2020 by Taylor & Francis Group, LLC
Routledge/Productivity Press is an imprint of Taylor & Francis Group, an Informa business

No claim to original U.S. Government works

Printed on acid-free paper

International Standard Book Number-13: 978-0-367-21849-2 (Hardback)
International Standard Book Number-13: 978-0-429-26650-8 (eBook)

Library of Congress Control Number: 2019948482

**Visit the Taylor & Francis Web site at
http://www.taylorandfrancis.com**

**and the CRC Press Web site at
http://www.crcpress.com**

Contents

Foreword

Project management has existed before the dawn of modern civilization; and zillions of projects have been initiated and executed since before language was created and certainly before MS Project was invented or the PMBOK, Agile, or CAM2P methodologies were authored. Any doubts? Then explain how were the Pyramids built or the Babylon Gardens were "hanged?"

In the later part of the 20th century, the ideology of project management and delivery process started taking shape. The project management institute (PMI) and similar organisations did a massive effort in developing the project manager (PM) field of practice as we know it today; and they "frameworked" the process and established it into a methodology for a booming profession.

Yet, with centuries of human expertise in managing and developing initiatives, statistics states that over 80% of projects still fail. How come we have written proven methodologies, and have super smart computers, software and (communicative) phones, yet projects still fail?

By instinct and logic, a previous mistake is avoided and best practice is repeated. This is a process of documenting lessons learned. Most often, PMs (if at all) gather those lessons learned to check a box within their firm's delivery process. But how many refer to those in their future projects or share them with other colleagues or organisations. I am tempted to say it is close to ZERO, as most of these documents go into the filing cabinet or the shredder after the contractual project period is over.

We are losing our ability to deliver value and quality, and losing our PRACTICAL tactics, which we gathered through decades of delivering projects!

Then comes this brilliant group of project case studies, originated from what was to be a desert within the Arabian Peninsula where massive projects were delivered in the last two decades. Dr S. Yusof and Dr K. Jaafar brilliantly compiled a collection of delivered projects from different industries, compiling the stories behind their risks and opportunities and best practices and mistakes for the PM community to learn from.

Having a process and methodology is great, but verifying it is even more important. In my opinion, *The Digital Project Management Evolution* is a must-read for all PMs or PMs to be with the desire to improve their project delivery outlook and learn about examples of pitfalls to avoid and best practices to follow and improve.

Lessons Learned…overdue!

Samer Mahdi MSc | PMP
Senior Capital Projects Manager Middle
East and Africa – General Electric

Preface

Over the past few years, many frameworks have been developed to help PMs run their projects effectively. Every framework has set processes for different project phases. According to recent research, despite all of the standards that have been set, more than 80% of projects fail. Failure usually means projects are out of scope, budget, or time. It is apparent that any standard being adopted can improve projects by minimising their deviations from specific set of targets, but that alone is not capable of making projects reach their objectives. In other words, they might improve project processes rather than setting the optimal one. It is apparent that there is no such unique project management standard that fits all types of projects. This lead to a valid argument that those standards always need to be benchmarked and updated with processes that have proven to be effective in the practical field.

The benchmark process needs to take into consideration many variables that are project-specific, and hence innovative and adaptive processes need to be tailored according to certain conditions. The fact that every project and industry has its specific enterprise environmental and organisational variables results in an extra challenge during any benchmarking and implementation process. United Arab Emirates in recent years has been exposed to a vast number of projects in different fields. Those projects fall under either derivative, platform, or breakthrough projects and hence different processes have been adopted by companies that were involved in the planning and implementation phases. Those companies are multinational and many of them are leaders in their fields.

Maybe the best way to learn project management, other than on-the-job training, is through case studies and circumstances. Project managers are proud to find solutions to problems, and case studies are a great way to do this. Case studies allow students to properly investigate what went right, what went wrong, and what suggestions should be made to avoid recurrence of these problems. The use of case studies applies both to project management courses at undergraduate and graduate levels as well as to training courses for passing project management certification exams.

The use of case studies has traditionally been emphasised in many fields of study. People use cases to illustrate building theory, testing theory, description, or even for simple explanation. Nevertheless, trying to learn has always been an ultimate goal in which we focus our attention on the severity of the problems and issues related to the case. Case studies are also one of the best tools often used for continuing education and career development in the project management field.

For the past few years, the PMI has encouraged many authors to write and develop case studies related to project management. The main idea is to utilise these cases as a means of speeding up the learning process for project management. There are stand-alone casebooks dedicated to project management. What is introspectively missing is a robust case study book that takes into consideration enterprise environmental factors (EEFs) that are region- and project-specific. We truly believe this book is one of the few practical initiatives to deal with managing projects from UAE-specific enterprise environmental process. The intent of this book is to enhance readers' learning experiences by using market-specific case studies. We believe such approach will enable readers to enhance their knowledge and understanding of project concepts and practices.

In trying to identify different aspects of project management, we edited 12 cases, each of which was raised by professionals with different expertise. We have used fictitious names in the cases to hide identities. These cases are credible since they reflect actual projects in different industries, with different project types and sizes. Our main objective is to showcase project management and organisational project management processes and industry practices in MENA market settings.

This book is customised for both experienced and inexperienced PMs. As you read this book, try taking each project and referencing the lessons learned that apply to you. The most active takeaways from the book are, as anyone might expect, "The Lessons Learned." Each project has, obviously, unexpected issues, the difficulties of which you can learn from. We realise that in each project there are difficulties and distinctive lessons learned. Applying these lessons is the key to improving PMs the second, third, and *n*th time around. This book is intended to address different groups and individuals with different priorities, including but not limited to:

Executives, programme managers, and PMs: This book will help enhance their project, programme, and organisational management knowledge and understanding.

Consultants and academics: This book is a good practical resource guide for PMs. For academics, it acts as a recommended accompanying reading for their project management classes. Students can make use of this book by adopting it as a reference or as a necessary text. The cases in this book can support any fundamental class textbooks on project management, programme management, or organisational project management. This book provides consultants with many real UAE project scenarios in which project frameworks were implemented.

CAPM®, PMP®, and PgMP® candidates: This book perfectly falls in line with PMI current standards and provides additional details necessary for certification purposes.

Excellence in project management for each individual arises from both theoretical and practical information and knowledge. In today's world of extreme competitiveness, any one of these frameworks standing alone would not be enough. We believe that this book will allow our readers to gain such diversified knowledge and learn from experiences shared by other practitioners in project management. All in all, this book simply captures various stories. We expect, however, that these relevant project scenarios will function as building blocks to drive excellence in project management.

Structure of this Book

This book offers a number of project case scenarios with various contextual investigations that aim to show the power of utilising project management practices. The contextual investigations highlight genuine project circumstances, challenges, and best practices adopted. In order for our readers to best learn from those cases, we have categorised and arranged our book chapters into different scenarios and problems. In Chapter 1, we introduced the field of project management from an historical perspective, highlighted the importance of the field and where it is heading with its risks and challenges. After this introductory chapter, we illustrated the different types of case studies involving different types of companies in detail. In the first case study, Chapter 2, the focus is on two of the key factors, which are communications and collaboration that has led to the success of a project. It is vital for a PM to communicate and collaborate effectively with all the team members and vendors who are involved in the project. This case study describes the challenges that the PM of Al Bukhary Inc. faced when the company was given the contract to build a three-tier data centre for Star Real Estates, which is the leading real estate company in the Middle East. In the second case study, Chapter 3, the purpose is to understand how a change request comes about, as well as the steps that are taken to implement it. Change requests are key elements of software maintenance and evolution. They may be small or large, depending on the needs of the organisation. To deal with change requests, the PM and project team members have a dedicated plan to follow, which is called a Change Request Management Plan. The third case study, Chapter 4, discusses how important is to collect information about the project before proceeding with the actual sign off to avoid wasting time and money. The new system was supposed to be used to improve one area while it highlighted several weaknesses like poor project communication, weak data requirements definition, and less awareness about the benefits of the project between the end users. The fourth case study, Chapter 5, is about how a company dealt with issues relating to multicultural differences existing among its workers. The PM had no experience working with a culturally diverse team and some changes needed to be made regarding the time frame for project completion, which needed to be reduced. This caused uneasiness and frequent fights among the workers. The fifth case study, Chapter 6, illustrates technology-related or rather specific vulnerabilities that are faced by managers when they make international trips related to their business dealings. It highlights the importance of handling technology and shows how critical it is for managers to adapt to technology in this era of global connectivity, which is related to the management of complex passwords and virtual protocol networks (VPNs). The sixth case study, Chapter 7, aims to tell a story about the implementation of an enterprise resource planning (ERP) system in a large company in the UAE. The purpose is to highlight the issues and formulate a list of the lessons learned during the project, as told by the Chief Information Officer (CIO) and the ERP PM. The seventh case study, Chapter 8, is about changes that were made to the project scope at the Elafifi Group. The IT project was to create an Elafifi management dashboard that would provide high-level performance indicators and business performance for the Elafifi companies. One of the objectives of having these dashboards was to enable all concerned heads of business and operations to benefit from them. The eighth case study, Chapter 9, examines from the PM's perspective and showcases the issues faced by the company, how it impacted multiple projects, and how the issues could be resolved based on the framework proposed in this research. In retrospect, vendor selection is a complex topic that is related to a request for proposal (RFP), request for quotation (RFQ), and negotiation. The ninth case study, Chapter 10, is about a project that was undertaken with the aim of migrating a bank's IT infrastructure from its premises to the cloud. The main reason for migrating the infrastructure to the cloud was to gain cloud benefits and to be able to access information from any location. The tenth case study, Chapter 11, demonstrates the implementation of a real-time interface between a new system and core banking system. The new system facilitates automatic account opening, posting, and limit checking, and it enables the user to read financial interest rates. The PM needs to consider proper change management; especially, if there will be a significant change in the user experience. The 11th case study, Chapter 12, discusses the Ministry of Society Advancement (MOSA) operation team, which was to conduct a comprehensive health check of the business environment and priorities of its business, as well as the technical requirements of its information system. The MOSA is a federal entity, which has its headquarters in Dubai, as well as social affairs and social development offices across the UAE. The last case study, Chapter 13, explores a project that was undertaken by two companies, MBI and the Artics, that ended in partial failure. The main objectives of the project were to develop an autonomous car that the teams can demonstrate and teach attendees how to develop themselves. However, no one was able to actually get a car up and running. Moreover, a misunderstanding happened between the two teams regarding the full functionality of the car. The case study examines the steps taken by both companies in order to prevent such failures in the future and improve on their collaboration process.

Case Types

The cases in this book are classified into three different types: critical events, problem-based cases, and comprehensive cases. The difference between these three categories is in terms of case length and specificity, which are described as follows:

■ Critical events are structured and written in the form of short stories illustrating issues and problems that are related to organisational project management.

- Problem-based cases are structured to offer more facts and evidence than critical incidents. They usually feature two or more issues either in project management, programme management, or organisational project management.
- Comprehensive cases are the lengthiest. They cover several problems or the entirety of the project, programme, or organisational project management.

The main objective behind writing cases of different levels is to offer readers a diversified set of learning skills. This way they can make use of this book to adapt their learning needs. In addition, this book has both open-ended cases, where we do not show the final outcomes of the story, and close-ended cases, where the final outcomes are presented for further discussion.

Dr Shafiz Affendi Mohd Yusof and Dr Kamal Jaafar
Dubai, June 2019

Acknowledgements

As professors teaching IT and engineering project management subjects, we always imagined that we could provide insights on project management in the context of Middle East. Indeed, our dreams have come true!

We would like to thank the writers and contributors of the chapters. The case studies are illuminating, inspirational, and enlightening, and encompass unique experiences and practices.

We would also like to thank our Dean of Faculty of Engineering and Information Sciences, Professor Dr Khalid Hussein for his support specifically, and UOWD generally.

We also would like to thank our families and friends for their endless encouragement.

Finally, we would like to dedicate this book to all future and current PMs. We hope the lessons learned from these case studies will empower you to be an agent of change through your innovative projects and esteemed leadership.

Dr Shafiz Affendi Mohd Yusof and Kamal Jaafar
University of Wollongong in Dubai

Editors

Dr Shafiz Affendi Mohd Yusof is an Associate Professor at the Faculty of Engineering and Information Sciences, University of Wollongong in Dubai. He is the Discipline Leader for Master of Information Technology Management (MITM) and Head of the Information Systems and Technology (INSTECH) Research Group. He holds a PhD in Information Science and Technology, MPhil in Information Transfer, MS in Telecommunications and Network Management from Syracuse University, and BS in Information Technology from University Utara Malaysia.

Dr Shafiz has 18 years of teaching experience at the undergraduate and postgraduate level. He teaches IT Project Management, Information Technology Strategic Planning, E-Business, System Analysis, and Research Methods. His teaching philosophy is based on the humanistic approach, which is based on exploring the self and instilling "fun" in the students in his classes. He feels that when students have fun, they tend to be comfortable and the information that is taught to them tends to remain in their long-term memory.

Dr Shafiz was previously a faculty member of School of Computing as Associate Professor in University Utara Malaysia. He held various other senior roles, including Director of International Telecommunication Union at Universiti Utara Malaysia Asia Pacific Centre of Excellence (ITU-UUM ASP CoE) for Rural Information and Communication Technologies (ICT) Development and Deputy Director of Cooperative and Entrepreneurship Development Institute (CEDI). He is a certified professional trainer (Train of Trainers' Programme) under the Ministry of Human Resource, Malaysia and has conducted several workshops on computers and ICT.

Dr Shafiz was awarded the "Excellence Service Award 2008" for his teaching, research, and administrative contributions to his university.

He was also awarded several research grants under several national and international bodies such as the Windows on Science (WOS) Program from the Asian Office of Aerospace Research & Development (AOARD), Japan; Ministry of Energy, Water and Communication (MEWC); Ministry of Higher Education (MED), Malaysia; and Malaysian Commission of Multimedia and Communications (MCMC). He was chosen to represent Malaysia in the Asian Pacific Economic Cooperation (APEC) Workshop on Embedding Entrepreneurship at University Curriculum in Hanoi, Vietnam (2008) to present a paper on Malaysia's initiatives on developing entrepreneurship programmes at institutes of higher learning.

Dr Shafiz's research interests focuses on the social impact of Information Technology, information behaviour, project management, virtual/e-community, e-government, teleworking, community networks, rural ICT, technopreneurship, and open source. He has published his works in refereed journals, conference papers, encyclopaedias, and book chapters. He has supervised the completion of 8 PhDs and over 70 MSc Students.

Dr Kamal Jaafar is an Associate Professor at the Faculty of Engineering and Information Sciences, University of Wollongong in Dubai. He is the Program Leader for the Master of Information Technology Management, Master of Engineering Management, and the Master of Engineering Asset Management.

He holds BS, MPhil, and PhD degrees in Engineering from the University of Cambridge and an MBA from the Ashcroft International Business School in Cambridge. He also undertook studies in international relations at Harvard University. He was honoured by Prince Charles as a Fellow of the Cambridge Overseas Trust. His research won first prize at the Royal College in London organised by KRSF. Dr Jaafar is a corporate consultant in Project Management.

Contributors

M. Abdulwadood Marashi
3M
Dubai, United Arab Emirates

Ishtiaq Ahmad
Emirates Airlines
Dubai, United Arab Emirates

Afrah Ahmed
Etisalat
Dubai, United Arab Emirates

Zakareya Alalawi
Social Care and Minors Affairs
    Foundation
Abu Dhabi, United Arab Emirates

Hessa Taha Alhaj Nasser
Ministry of Community of
    Development
Dubai, United Arab Emirates

Lama Al-Ibaisi
Optimum Partners
Dubai, United Arab Emirates

Mohammad Nabil Arif
Magnitt
Dubai, United Arab Emirates

Bilal Jamshed Butt
Pakistan Railways
Lahore, Pakistan

Jan Michael De Villeres
Dubai Courts
Dubai, United Arab Emirates

Moon Diab
BMW
Dubai, United Arab Emirates

Mohamed Dib
Bank of Sharjah
Sharjah, United Arab Emirates

Jean Edmond El Kesserwani
CG Technology LLC
Dubai, United Arab Emirates

Abdullah El Nokiti
British University of Dubai
Dubai, United Arab Emirates

Kevin Francis
Kernel Technologies
Dubai, United Arab Emirates

Kanika Gambhir
Silicus Technologies
Dubai, United Arab Emirates

Mariam Hamad
Ministry of Education
Dubai, United Arab Emirates

Kimmy Hanspal
Market-i
Dubai, United Arab Emirates

Yasmeen Hassan
GForces Web Management
Dubai, United Arab Emirates

Hazem Hussein
InfoVista
Dubai, United Arab Emirates

Fayyaz Imtiaz
Ingram Micro
Dubai, United Arab Emirates

Masood Iqbal
University of Wollongong in Dubai
Dubai, United Arab Emirates

Kiren Jackie
University of Wollongong in Dubai
Dubai, United Arab Emirates

Chandni Joshi
Chronometer General Trading
Dubai, United Arab Emirates

**Harish Ramanujam
Krishnaswani**
Wirecard Processing
Dubai, United Arab Emirates

Aoun Lutfi
IBM
Dubai, United Arab Emirates

Mohammed Abdul Mateen
Seddiqi Holding
Dubai, United Arab Emirates

Aditi Mishra
Careem
Dubai, United Arab Emirates

Aisha Khalifa Mohamed
Ministry of Community of
    Development
Dubai, United Arab Emirates

Khawla Mubarak
Emirates Airlines
Dubai, United Arab Emirates

Yasmine Al Najar
University of Wollongong in Dubai
Dubai, United Arab Emirates

Pranav Patil
StarLink
Dubai, United Arab Emirates

Shweta Rajderkar
Leap Dev
Sydney, Australia

Ali Rezaei
University of Wollongong in Dubai
Dubai, United Arab Emirates

Mohammad Al Sammach
Dubai Police
Dubai, United Arab Emirates

Sameer Malik Shaik
Emirates Global Aluminium
Dubai, United Arab Emirates

Suzan Shaker
University of Wollongong in Dubai
Dubai, United Arab Emirates

Abdullah Siddiq
Ajman University
Ajman, United Arab Emirates

Sheeba Sonia
Jumbo Electronics
Dubai, United Arab Emirates

Bilkisu Aminu Suleiman
Tertiary Education Trustfund
(Tetfund)
Abuja, Nigeria

Muhammad Faizzan Zafar
Emmar
Dubai, United Arab Emirates

Basl Ali Zam
Etisalat
Dubai, United Arab Emirates

Hamda Al Zarooni
University of Wollongong in Dubai
Dubai, United Arab Emirates

Chapter 1

Project Management Evolution: From Traditional to Responsive Project Management

Kamal Jaafar and Shafiz Affendi Mohd Yusof
University of Wollongong in Dubai

Contents

Project management is a topic that has been and is still being excessively discussed. Modern project management dates back to the 19th century, when Henry Gantt developed techniques for planning and controlling projects, such as the widely used Gantt chart. The growth of modern project management in the 19th century came as a consequence of the necessity of structured manufacturing, transportation, and construction industries.

This being said, it can be deduced that one of the major industries that contributed to the birth of project management is the construction industry. Because of their complex nature, construction projects need to be managed in a flexible manner; projects related to construction are usually large and enlist numerous functions and disciplines. Additionally, they tend to be unpredictable in their nature; no two construction projects are identical.

Another industry whose projects are unpredictable and require flexibility in management is the software development or IT industry. During the 1990s, developers of software in the information technology industry became concerned with the current techniques of project management. Their main concern lay in the fact that projects are traditionally planned under the assumption that they are predictable. Whereas, in reality, unforeseen changes tend to occur in almost every project executed to date. Inability to accommodate such changes leads to a waste of time and resources. Hence, traditional project management techniques can be problematic for projects such as IT or construction projects.

In order to handle this issue, different project management approaches have been developed. Many of the existing approaches incorporate sets of techniques to manage changes and to keep the project flexible should any abrupt changes come up. In other words, many of those approaches treat the project as if it is unpredictable. Hence, the planning and execution differs from traditional methods.

The key elements of responsive project management should include client interaction, team integration, and flexibility. This is achieved by iterative development as also seen in Figure 1.1. Hence, responsive project management is all about attaining flexibility by being able to adapt to any

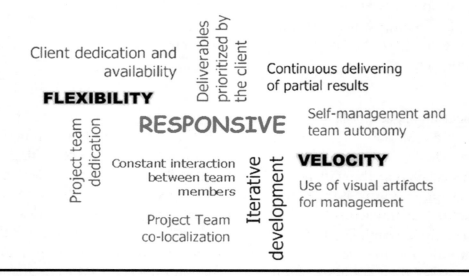

Figure 1.1   Key elements of responsive project management approach.

unforeseen changes in order to deliver the best possible outcome for client satisfaction. In addition, it involves increased client participation and input throughout different project stages.

As mentioned earlier, most responsive project management approaches are primarily developed for software development projects. However, recent research is being oriented towards extending it beyond the scope of the IT sector.

1.1 Application Gap

In an extensive study conducted by Conforto's Global Survey, 60% of the studied projects were found to be using the traditional project management approach, and 28% were found to be using some form of responsive methods, 7% used hybrid techniques and 4% used "other" methods. The latter being referred to methods used internally by the company (Conforto, Rebentisch, & Amaral, 2014). These findings, combined with the fact that out of 856 responses only 11 are from the UAE, serve as evidence to the significance of investigating project management approaches being adopted in UAE projects.

1.2 Responsive Project Management Beyond IT and Software Development Industry

As mentioned earlier, the global survey carried out by Conforto et al. (2014) did prove the existence of a gap in the implementation of responsive practices in many industry and business segments.

Responsive project management enablers are defined as "internal or external factors to the organisation that are directly or indirectly related with the implementation of the project management approach that may impact the performance and use of a given practice, technique, or tool." The following four values are key elements that need to be considered when adopting a responsive approach in managing projects: (1) "Individuals and interactions over processes and tools"; (2) "Working software over comprehensive documentation"; (3) "Customer collaboration over contract negotiation"; and (4) "Responding to change over following a plan."

As mentioned earlier, the rationale behind responsiveness in project management is realising that projects are not predictable in nature.

Throughout the lifetime of the project, there are changes in market or in the product itself, in addition to other unforeseen changes. Since rational responsive project management practices divide a large project into smaller chunks, it becomes easier to prioritise or add or drop any feature in the middle of the project life cycle. Whereas in traditional projects where excessive upfront planning is done, unforeseen changes tend to have considerable impacts on project schedule. Hence, it is recommended that the following steps be adopted in the project management approach: (1) flexibility and iterative development; (2) project team dedication; (3) client dedication and availability; and (4) team autonomy and self-management.

The above enablers should be adopted on the following levels: organisation, process, project team, and project type. On the other hand, there are critical barriers to responsive implementation, those barriers can be summarised as follows: (1) changing mindset to allow flexibility; (2) long-term planning; and (3) poor process visibility.

1.3 Responsive Project Management Challenges and Risks

A key element of responsive project management is autonomy and self-organising project teams. However, this comes at a price. In a brief manner, the following challenges will be encountered across following levels:

- Task Level: Lack of acceptance criteria and task dependency
- Individual Level: Asserting autonomy and self-assignment
- Team Level: Achieving cross-functionality and effective estimations
- Project Level: Delayed and changing requirements and senior management sponsorship

Some recommendations to overcome or address such challenges are as follows:

- Planning with a holistic approach
- Sharing knowledge to attain cross-functionality
- Effective means of communication
- Investment in technology
- Considering the role of the responsive project manager

In short, today's project management approaches provide the foundation for any type of other adequate approaches to be combined upon them for any specific projects especially IT projects to be worked on. This is because IT projects are dynamic in nature and require an approach that is responsive in nature and agile in methodology. For example, during the beginning phase, a traditional approach can be adopted and during the implementation phase, a more responsive approach could be used (Jovanovic & Beric, 2018). Furthermore, it gives an advantage for the project manager and for the project team the choice on the best approaches and most suitable direction towards completing a project successfully.

References

Conforto, E.C., Rebentisch, E., & Amaral, D.C., 2014. *Project Management Agility Global Survey*. Cambridge, MA: Massachusetts Institute of Technology, Consortium for Engineering Program Excellence (CEPE).

Jovanovic, P., & Beric, I., 2018. Analysis of the available project management methodologies. *Journal of Sustainable Business and Management Solutions in Emerging Economies*, 23, 1–13.

Chapter 2

Communication and Collaboration: The Key Factors to Project Management

Afrah Ahmed
Etisalat

Mohammed Abdul Mateen
Seddiqi Holding

Hazem Hussein
InfoVista

Mariam Hamad
Ministry of Education

Contents

2.1 Introduction

"We have to launch the data centre by the end of this month. This project cannot be delayed any further," said Bosco during his weekly meeting with his team.

Bosco joined Al Bukhary Inc. 9 years ago as a project engineer and is now the head of the Project Management team. During his tenure at the company, he has led numerous successful projects, regardless of how challenging they have seemed.

He always motivates his team by saying, "Nothing is impossible. The word 'impossible' itself says 'I'm possible.'"

However, the project they have been working on for the past 4 months has been a complete "head scratcher." It was supposed to be completed within 3 months; however, it has been 4 months, and the project is still ongoing.

Star Real Estates wanted to build a three-tier certified data centre, as it did not have one. Therefore, the company hired Al Bukhary Inc. and many other vendors to build a data centre that would include passive work, such as raised floors, structured cabling, racks, cooling units, and fire-prevention systems, as well as active components, which would include network devices, servers, and storage units. The challenge in the project was not the installation of the new components; rather, it was the migration of Star Real Estates' existing systems, such as Microsoft Exchange, the enterprise resource planning (ERP) system, and file servers. Star Real Estates wanted multiple system integrators to work together to undertake this project.

As the project manager, Bosco had to coordinate with all the technical teams related to the systems that were to be integrated and deployed at the data centre to develop one big solution for Star Real Estates.

"I don't know what to do, John. This is one of the most challenging projects I have ever handled. The customer has so many unrealistic expectations, and dealing with all the system integrators …God! They don't even cooperate," said Bosco to John, the technical leader of his team.

2.2 Organisational Background – The Journey to Success: From 5 to 500

Al Bukhary Inc. is a leading information and communication technology (ICT) company in the Middle East. It started out with five employees in 1984 and has over 500 today. The company is now the market leader in the

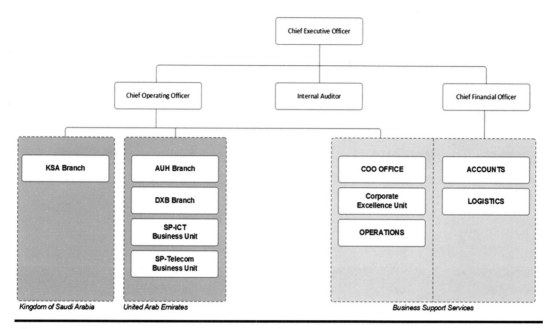

Figure 2.1   Strategic business unit block diagram for Al Bukhary Inc.

provision of ICT solutions in the Middle East, as it is the leading partner to numerous ICT heavyweights, such as CISCO, F5, Dell, and Palo Alto. The company constantly contributes to nation building, which has placed it at the top of the ICT partners list (Figure 2.1).

Al Bukhary Inc. has offices in the UAE and KSA, which currently cover the entire Middle East. Figure 2.2 depicts a detailed organisational chart that shows how a specific branch of Al Bukhary Inc. operates. It consists of four main departments: sales, presales, service delivery, and operations. The implementation and project management teams come under the Service Delivery Department; hence, there is one service delivery manager for each branch. The Sales and Presales Department of each branch has its own specific managers, who, along with the service delivery manager, report to the branch manager, who then reports to the COO of Al Bukhary Inc.

Al Bukhary Inc.'s corporate vision is to offer and provide the best quality in ICT infrastructure solutions to its customers at a competitive price. The company's mission includes the following:

■ To provide cost-effective and quality solutions to its customers based on their defined practices
■ To provide and adhere to strict quality policies in its daily operations, in which it is ISO certified

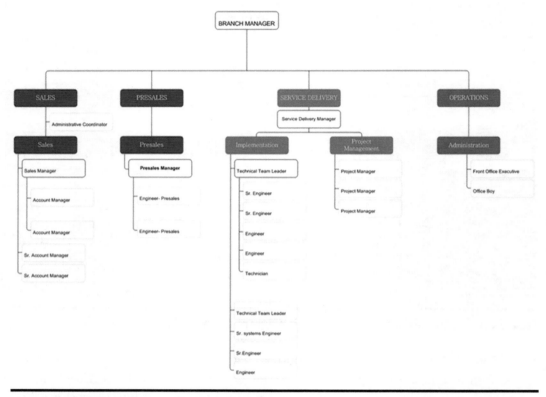

Figure 2.2   Detailed Al Bukhary Inc. organisational chart.

■ To follow ethical standards regardless of whom the company is dealing with—that is, whether customers, partners, or employees
■ To empower, reward, and recognise its employees
■ To create a positive work environment

Al Bukhary Inc. takes pride in and believes in the continuous improvement of its internal processes, which form the base of its operations. Hence, it empowers employees to provide feedback regarding possible improvements to the existing processes.

2.3 Case Description

2.3.1 Growth: Escalations . . . Escalations . . .

As Star Real Estates was the leading real estate company in the Middle East, all the system integrators had their best employees (i.e. the team leaders) involved in this project. Al Bukhary Inc. was responsible for carrying out all the passive work for the three-tier data centre. One of the passive components was the CCU, which keeps the data centre cool, and it was supposed to be delivered by a well-known electric company called XYZ Electrics, whose salesperson promised to deliver the product to the site within 6 weeks. It had now been 7 weeks, and Linda who is responsible in sales and John were discussing the projects with which they had been involved.

Linda said, "Are you serious? The CCU has not been delivered yet? They said they would deliver it last week. Bosco must be panicking!"

John replied, "Oh no. Bosco has amazing planning skills; he knew he had to have a buffer. So, he allocated 10 weeks for the expected delivery of the CCU."

Linda replied, "Oh, that's great! But I think you need to follow up with them. I have a meeting now; so, I have to rush. Let me know if you need help."

She then rushed out of the lounge. Based on Bosco's 10-week timeline, all the other system integrators submitted their plans to deliver the hardware, as well as their migration plans for the active components.

After finishing his coffee, John decided to call the senior implementation manager (IM) of XYZ Electrics to follow up on the delivery of the CCU. He said, "I don't understand what is causing the delay! You guys really need to deliver the CCU as promised. Otherwise, we will be in a big mess!"

The senior IM replied, "It will be delivered to the site in 3 weeks. Don't worry!" He then hung up.

John knew that XYZ Electrics was not taking him seriously and that it would probably not adhere to the agreed-upon timeline. Three weeks passed, and the CCU had not been delivered; therefore, John decided to speak to Bosco about it. He immediately went to Bosco's office and informed him of the situation. Bosco asked him to call the senior IM once again. Bosco then asked John to contact him after speaking with the senior IM.

John called XYZ Electrics and said, "It's been 3 weeks since we had the call, and there is still no sign of the CCU! What is the point of agreements if you cannot keep your commitments? Do you know the position we are in because of this?"

After a heated conversation with XYZ Electrics, John updated Bosco about the phone call. Bosco knew that he had to get involved, as the situation was getting out of hand.

He, therefore, decided to call the assistant vice president (AVP) of XYZ Electrics, to whom he stated, "We have given multiple orders to your company, and such delays cannot be tolerated. This could jeopardise all of our future transactions."

The AVP replied, "Don't worry. I will look into it. Your CCU will be delivered soon."

Despite Bosco's buffer and his call to the AVP, events did not unfold as planned. The project began to unravel when one of the system integrators told the IT project manager at Star Real Estates that "it's not professional on Al Bukhary Inc.'s part to not deliver the hardware within the agreed time frame. I mean, if they couldn't adhere to this deadline, why did they make such a commitment?"

The IT project manager asked, "How late are they?" to which the system integrator replied, "Two weeks. We could have finished a lot in 2 weeks."

The IT project manager knew that he would be held responsible for the delay; therefore, instead of speaking to Bosco and inquiring about the delay, he decided to escalate the issue to the CIO of Star Real Estates. The CIO was furious about the delay, as this project was very important. He decided to talk to Al Bukhary Inc.'s COO, whom he called immediately and to whom he said the following:

"We hired you because we thought you were the best in the region. These unjustified delays are unacceptable! Every time we call you, we get a new excuse and a new deadline that is not met! Do you know how much is at stake for us?"

"I understand, but the electric company we hired has been delaying the delivery. You can ask your IT manager; we have been meeting all his expectations—even the new requirements he added."

"I don't care about that! The CCU was always a part of the requirements of the project, and it is still not there on the site. How are we supposed to operate a data centre without a CCU? The entire project has been delayed by 3 weeks! Even the quality of the cable work is terrible!"

The COO attempted to convince the CIO that the former's company was not responsible for the delay, but the CIO was livid and was unwilling to try to understand anything that he was being told. Consequently, the COO concluded the conversation by saying, "I understand. I will keep a close watch on the project and make sure everything is delivered on time. You will not face any further delays from our side."

After the phone call, the COO called Bosco and told him, "Get this project completed as soon as possible. Do whatever they want. And I want daily updates on this!"

2.3.2 Damage Control

The COO knew that the damage had already been done and that the only way out of the mess in which the company had found itself was to complete the project at the earliest. Therefore, he called the AVP of XYZ Electrics and said, "Marc, we are doing business here! If you want us to place any future orders with your company, instruct your team to deliver the CCU in the next 6 days. I cannot tolerate these delays anymore!"

After the phone call, the COO of Al Bukhary Inc. and the AVP of XYZ Electrics had an emergency meeting to normalise the relationship between the two teams. The AVP knew that Al Bukhary Inc. was one of his company's biggest clients and that if the CCU was delayed any further, they would lose a significant amount of business. Hence, he made sure that his team worked diligently to deliver the CCU on time. The CCU was delivered to the site before the end of the 6 days that the COO had given XYZ Electrics.

Despite the delivery of the CCU, Al Bukhary Inc. knew that it would take considerably more to make its customer happy; the company had to "go above and beyond." Bosco ensured that he updated the COO on a daily basis, regardless of how small or insignificant the update seemed. Moreover, they made a few rational decisions, such as changing the cabling vendor to ensure better quality and flexibility of the cables to meet the customer's expectations. Furthermore, they had to make immediate design decisions, as this was one of the biggest concerns of Star Real Estates and was one of the reasons why they had kept delaying the approval of the proposed design. As a result of the escalation to the CIO and COO, the decisions and approvals were sped up to make up for the time that had been lost during the initial stage of the project.

2.3.3 Identification of the Root Cause

Being one of the leading system integrators in the region, Al Bukhary Inc. took the project delay very seriously. After completing the project for Star Real Estates, the COO of Al Bukhary Inc. asked Bosco to find the root cause of the problem. Therefore, Bosco and his team had a meeting with XYZ Electrics to discuss the cause of the delay.

During the meeting, Bosco was shocked when the senior IM told him, "I sincerely apologise for the delay. It was a miss on our part. We shouldn't have allowed Sam to handle the initial a request for proposal (RFP) alone, because he was serving his notice period." Bosco's facial expression changed, and it became evident that the situation caused him to question the integrity of XYZ Electrics. To reassure him, the senior IM added the following:

"We have blacklisted Sam in our records and changed our process of handling the request for proposals (RFPs) to ensure that employees in their notice periods have to keep their managers involved in all external communications. In addition, the employee's manager will allocate a resource person to shadow the employee who will be leaving the company soon. Human Resources (HR) has also been informed to communicate with the concerned employee's department head as soon as they receive any formal resignation from the employee, wherein the department head was not copied. This is to ensure that the department head can, in turn, take appropriate actions to shadow the employee. I can assure you that this will not happen again!"

After Bosco had an understanding of the situation, was convinced that it had been a mishap, and felt that it would not be repeated, he wrapped up the meeting with XYZ Electrics.

After heading back to his office, Bosco had a meeting with his team, during which he said to his service delivery manager, "You know what? It didn't cross my mind earlier, but I should have asked for Sam during the initial escalation which was done by John in week 7."

After further discussions, John admitted that instead of following up with the electric company verbally, he should have sent emails mentioning the 6-week deadline that Sam had initially promised for the delivery of the CCU. It was evident that the root cause of the delay had been miscommunication and that immediate measures had to be taken. Bosco concluded the meeting by instructing his team members to follow up via email to ensure that they have evidence in case there is a similar occurrence in the future. He added, "Let's have another meeting tomorrow and develop a process for communicating with our vendors."

2.4 Solutions and Recommendations

In regard to multi-vendor projects, one of the most critical challenges that must be addressed is communication with project stakeholders. This is one of the factors that can contribute to the success or the failure of a project (Aaltonen, 2011). Because projects move in a dynamic way throughout their life cycles, this creates a dynamic context in which the project stakeholders must be managed in each phase. Examining the modes of communication that are used with different project stakeholders ensures that there is effective engagement among them, and this plays a fundamental role in the success of the project. The study concluded that it is mandatory to determine the perceived salience of each stakeholder group and accordingly ascertain whether to communicate using an impersonal mode or personal and group modes (Turkilainen, Aaoltonen, & Lohikoski, 2015). Regarding the case study, there was a lack of formal communication between the different vendors with regard to updates about their plans and timelines. This led to an unexpected delay, and therefore, no previous warning was provided by Al Bukhary Inc. to other system integrators.

Multi-vendor projects can be categorised as programmes that arise from the need to have an effective mechanism for governing the projects. A research study was conducted to facilitate and improve communication across different project teams and vendors, and the results showed that using contact centres improved collaboration and communication across different teams. The use of contact centres enhanced the deliverables, satisfaction, and service delivery (Bond-Barnard & Steyn, 2013). Star Real Estates should have built such a centre to facilitate communication between the different vendors and opened a formal communication channel between them to enable them to synchronise their activities, update their plans, and share the risks associated with their actions.

Scholars have also investigated the effect of team integration and group cohesion on project performance and delivery time. The studies have shown that team integration leads to lower costs, closer adherence to schedules, and higher quality (Franz, Leicht, Molenaar, & Messner, 2017). In the above case, Star Real Estates' IT project manager should have taken the initiative to call all the system integrators together for a meeting, during which he should have urged them to work as a team and emphasised the importance of team integration and group cohesion.

2.5 Lesson Learned Questions

- What was the main problem in the case?
- Is it only the system integrator (ABC) who needs to ponder on what went wrong? If yes/no, justify your answer.
- If you were in the shoes of the IT project manager of Star Real Estate Company, how differently you would have handled the delay in the project?

References

Aaltonen, K. (2011). Project stakeholder analysis as an environmental interpretation process. *International Journal of Project Management*, 29(2), 165–183.

Bond-Barnard, T.J., & Steyn, H. (2013). The programme benefits of improving project team communication through a contact centre. *South African Journal of Industrial Engineering*, 24, 127–139.

Franz, B., Leicht, R., Molenaar, K., & Messner, J. (2017). Impact of team integration and group cohesion on project delivery performance. *Journal of Construction Engineering & Management*, 143, 1–12.

Turkilainen, V., Aaoltonen, K., & Lohikoski, P. (2015). Managing project stakeholder communication: the qstock festival case. *Project Management Journal*, 46, 74–91.

Chapter 3

Change Request Management and Best Practices in IngeniousTec IT Project Management

Kiren Jackie
University of Wollongong in Dubai

Lama Al-Ibaisi
Optimum Partners

Suzan Shaker
University of Wollongong in Dubai

Yasmeen Hassan
GForces Web Management

Contents

3.1 Introduction

"Hello . . . Hi Marc," Anita answered.

"Hi, Anita! Please stop the website launch! We can't go live now!" Marc stated.

"Why? What's wrong? We already started the launching process," Anita replied.

"We need to change the page layout and remove the new model pages. Let's discuss this tomorrow in the meeting," Marc responded before ending the call.

Change is the only constant in this world, but we need to embrace and learn from it to keep moving ahead. This was not a regular day; it was the day that the longest project that Anita had ever worked on would be launched. She prepared herself for all sorts of things possibly going wrong: software defects, software bugs, missing codes, or styling issues. However, this call from Marc was the last thing that Anita had expected to receive today. Everyone in the office went quiet and watched her as she rushed outside the office. This was not good news. I immediately followed Anita outside, as I had been assigned to be her co-pilot on this project management journey.

"What happened? What did Marc say?" I asked eagerly.

"Is he joking?! Is he seriously joking?" Anita replied. "He wants us to re-change the new vehicle pages layout AGAIN!"

"Is that even allowed?" I asked.

"Apparently, it is!" Anita replied nervously while walking back to her office.

For the past 4 months, I have been working with Anita as a junior project manager (PM). I graduated 2 years ago and joined IngeniousTec as a PHP developer, a position that I held for 1 year. However, I later discovered my passion for project management. I, therefore, took a project management course to enable me to pursue this career path. I decided to start my career path at IngeniousTec because it is one of the leading providers of Internet software and services in the automotive industry and helps to promote and sell vehicles through the use of digital mobile technologies and media.

I wanted to learn all that Anita knew, including how she dealt with big, complex projects. I was excited when I first learned that I would be assigned to work with her, as she holds a master's degree in marketing and has been a PM for 10 years. Before joining IngeniousTec, she worked as a consultant at one of the big four companies. Anita is well known for being dedicated to her work and punctual with regard to all of her appointments and meetings. After working with Anita for a few months, I have also noticed that she is open minded but has a bad memory. Because of her forgetfulness, she always carries a small notebook with her. From Anita's point of view, the main traits of an effective PM are extensive knowledge and experience in the field that he or she is managing. Additionally, a successful PM should be organised, action-oriented, and flexible, while possessing excellent management, estimation, leadership, and communication skills. Another main reason for my excitement was that I was eager to be part of one of the biggest and longest projects that was being executed by the company, which was the one to which Anita had been assigned as the PM.

3.2 Organisational Background

IngeniousTec is one of the leading providers of Internet software and services in the automotive industry and helps to promote and sell vehicles through the use of digital mobile technologies and media. IngeniousTec works with major car manufacturers in the United Kingdom and Europe, as well as the Middle East. The company is headquartered in the United Kingdom and has three additional offices in different countries, thereby enabling it to manage its clients worldwide. The company's mission is to help its clients navigate the complex online environment and develop marketing strategies to meet the various challenges that it encounters. By encouraging a digital-oriented focus, the company also helps its clients to nurture sustainable and productive online relationships with their customers.

As Europe's largest specialist automotive digital agency, IngeniousTec is committed to ensuring that its clients are able to use the digital environment to its full potential. Its in-house-developed software suite and automotive data services enable vehicle manufacturers and automotive retailers to manage their digital dealerships and vehicle stock using sector-specific technology. From Web through to showroom and aftersales systems, IngeniousTec can provide next-generation customer experience management and business insight at all levels of the automotive retail process via desktop, mobile, and tablet devices.

3.3 Case Description

This project is being undertaken in collaboration with a leading UAE client, which has been working with the company for a few years and for whom Anita has completed several successful projects in the past. For this project, the client requested to develop a group site that would connect all of its brand sites, act as the main destination for its customers, and inform them about all the client's services and offerings. The main stakeholders were identified: the marketing manager, Marc, and the marketing director, Sam. On the company side, the people who were directly involved were the PM, Anita; the programme manager, Lewis; and the account director, Robert. At the beginning of the project, the requirements were set and agreed upon. The PM reviewed all the requirements and provided feedback, as well as information about costs and timelines. The scope was set, and the work—which involved eight teams, development, QA, projects, CSS, design, UX, and software support—was started.

During the development of the group site, the main stakeholder kept making several change requests (CRs). He repeatedly changed his mind, regarding the way in which he wanted things to be done, thereby resulting in major changes and four redesign requests being made before the final website even went live. The budget that had been set kept changing throughout the project life cycle, which resulted in a great deal of frustration for Anita and all the team members who were involved as the project requirements and scope kept changing.

The stakeholder was indecisive and was unable to stick to one decision. Additionally, because of their desire to maintain their long relationship with the company, the executive board members accepted and escalated the changes to allow the PM to implement most of them. However, they had to reduce the profit margin and approve a few changes free of cost to get the website up and running. This required a free-of-charge (FOC) approval sign-off sheet, which can be signed by the company director only.

Finally, the project went live in April 2017, which was 16 months after the initial live date that had been set at the beginning of the project. No significant profit was made from this project, and the company decided to proceed in the interest of goodwill.

As this was part of my learning journey, we decided to have a "lessons learned" session after the project went live. Anita started the session by taking all attendees through the process that the company follows for any project in general, after which, she explained the challenges that she had faced with regard to this project, how they could have been avoided, and the specific types of issues or requests that had arisen. She compared the project to another similar one that was being undertaken simultaneously, and she mentioned the differences between each project stakeholder and how they set their requirements.

Anita explained that at the beginning, there are individuals from each department who will be working on only projects—not live sites. Therefore, whenever a project is set and the dates are confirmed, resources are booked and assigned based on this timeline. For any project, a 2-week buffer is always added; this is merely to provide time in which to go through the website, QA, and testing before handing the project over or going live on any website. Once the website is live, there is another 2-week process, which is essentially the time in which website performance is monitored, any unexpected gaps or issues are fixed, and all snags are delivered and closed. Once all of this is complete, the website is handed over to the Support Department, which will take care of any client requests ahead; this is when the project is officially closed.

For this specific project, the main issue that Anita faced was the number of CRs made by the stakeholders.

Anita stated, "when the CR comes during the project phase, the same team members will usually work on it, as they are assigned for the whole project-phase duration. However, for this case, the individuals working on the project kept changing, as the life span of the project got extended much further than the initial date."

As a common practice, the PM with the functional manager tends to assign the change to the same employee who worked on the feature or problem at the beginning; this is because all elements of such websites and technologies are related, and any change might affect another aspect of the website. Therefore, assigning the same resource person means that numerous other issues can be avoided, as he or she already knows all the dependencies. The figure below illustrates developers' most commonly used practices with regard to assignments in cases in which CRs are made (Figure 3.1).

Anita was asked to discuss the main CRs that were raised and how she dealt with them. Firstly, the enquiry form for the new field setup and mapping were submitted to an external third party. Secondly, the redesign of the platform was undertaken. This was a major change, as it put the platform on hold, required returning to the start by initiating the design phase again, and then going through cascading style sheets (CSS), then quality assurance (QA),

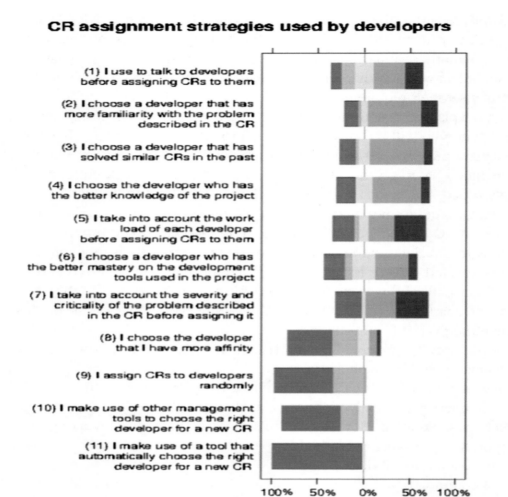

Figure 3.1   CR assignment strategies (Cavalcantia et al., 2016).

and so on. Thirdly, the new model pages were created. At the beginning of the project, Anita had advised the client against creating new pages, as this was duplicating data and work and would affect search engine optimization (SEO). Anita advised linking the models to the brand sites instead. However, the client had insisted on creating separate pages for the group site, and this request had been granted. Anita had received the final sign-off and they had agreed on the live date for the website. On launch day, the site had been set to go live. However, Marc had called Anita and requested that all the work be stopped, as he had decided to remove the new model pages from the site, as he had been advised to do at the beginning of the project, and to instead redirect and link them to the brand pages. This had caused the project to be delayed for 1 week.

For all the CRs raised, Anita followed the procedure. She explained to the client that this was a CR, as well as the factors that would be affected by the change. A project variation request document was created and signed by the stakeholder before starting to implement the change.

In contrast, well-run projects appear to be almost effortless; however, a great deal of work goes into running a project well. Project managers should strive to make their jobs easy to reflect the results of well-run projects. This specific case was an enterprise project delivery of a redesigned Al Jaabar Motors website. The website was intended to be a platform that provides users in the region with the ability to purchase a vehicle online for the first time and to do so while undergoing a 360° visualiser experience.

Anita considered it one of her best projects, and she was excited when talking about it, because it was completely new to this market and they wanted to take the lead. The project was also combined with a big campaign, was a massive undertaking, and had numerous eyes on it.

From the beginning, the client, Chris, was very "switched on" and he had a clear idea of exactly what they wanted. They provided clear requirements and were supportive of the feedback that was received from Anita. A scoping session was conducted, during which Anita reviewed all the requirements and provided feedback regarding the best approaches to undertake the project.

The client mentioned when they were planning to go live with the project, and based on this, it was divided into two phases to accommodate the agreed-upon date for going live. A Statement of Work document, which includes the process that will be followed, communication plan, risk plan, and breakdown of the scope, was prepared and submitted as a reference for both parties. The client reviewed and amended any requirements before signing off the project, after which the project was started. During the project execution phase, a few changes arose; however, they were all under control and did not affect the delivery time. Moreover, the client was ready to commit to any additional costs.

One of the main challenges of this project was overcoming technical matters related to third-party payment-process integration, the management of CRs with regard to the design templates, and content flow. As the third-party agencies were not involved since the start of the project, few issues arose during the integration phase, such as integrating finance payments and interest-rate calculations for the online payment provider.

Another time-consuming and challenging issue was the design template for the content flow. At the beginning of the project agreement, the client agreed on a specific design template; however, during the execution phase, the client was unfortunately unable to provide the required assets to apply for the agreed-upon design, which required a template change to adopt the assets that were available from the client. However, Anita believes that both of these challenges could have been avoided if the third party had been involved with the client during the planning phase and the client had been fully aware of their assets, resources, and limitations.

3.4 Solutions and Recommendations

After the session was over, I wanted to document my findings and analyse how improvements could be made by providing recommendations and best practices for future projects. During the project cycle, I continually monitored Anita's activities on our company's shared intranet, keeping track of every log she wrote about, as well as her thoughts on it. She frequently shared her ideas, even when she was disappointed about clients or new items. She also posted on the site whenever everyone was helpful with regard to suggestions and willingly shared ideas. Although the client caused a great deal of frustration, I believe that Anita made some mistakes as well. I think that because she was the only senior PM in the branch office, she was occupied with an overwhelming amount of work related to different clients and projects.

This workload caused immense pressure to be placed on her. In addition to planning and managing her work projects, Anita was planning her wedding, which heaped even more pressure on her shoulders. While attending a few meetings with Anita, I also noticed that she would sometimes argue with the client, insisting that her point of view was correct, solely to avoid having to make any changes to the scope, even if such changes were valid and would add value to the project. To avoid such incidents in future projects, I recommend dividing the workload into smaller milestones and giving the client a specific time frame within which to submit a CR before progressing to the next step. It would also be beneficial if the initial contract or scope entitled the client to a total of five FOC CRs, provided they do not exceed a preset value. This way the client is able to use these requests wisely and is unlikely to raise any issues unless doing so is necessary. The client will tend to save any requests until the end of the project in case they are needed, and it, therefore, becomes less likely that they will be used.

Additionally, a systemic change management plan should be formulated to minimise service downtime by ensuring that CRs are recorded, evaluated, authorised, prioritised, planned, tested, implemented, documented, and then reviewed in a controlled and consistent manner. Because the context information is dynamic, we should have clear CR assignment mechanisms that enable the assignment rules to evolve effortlessly, in keeping with changes in the context activities. We should also establish a specific structure that enables the acceptance of major changes. A full assortment and detailed brief with all involved parties will need to be undertaken, during which they will prototype the requests and confirm whether they are worth the money and effort required to complete them. Additionally, the ways in which this will or will not benefit the project, will be examined. We should also keep track of all requests and attempt to examine them in depth, as this might make the way for future opportunities for us as a company. According to Portny (2011), the following are the best CR management practices:

- As soon as a request is received, it should be acknowledged that it is a CR, and there should be a clarification regarding exactly what is being requested.
- The individual who is making the request must confirm in writing exactly what is being requested.
- In a formal change-control system, individuals must submit each CR on a CR form.
- The potential effects of the change on all aspects of the project must be evaluated.
- If the change will affect other individuals, they should be involved in the decision.
- If the decision is made to reject the change, the individual who has made the request should be informed, and the reason(s) for the denial should be explained to him or her.
- The project plan should be updated to reflect any adjustments to schedules, outcomes, or resource budgets, resulting from the change.
- Team members and appropriate audiences must be informed about the change and the effects that it is expected to have on the project.
- A risk assessment of the implementation of the change should be performed.
- Both time and budget buffers should be incorporated into the project plans.

3.5 Lessons Learned Questions

- What was the main problem in the case?
- What were the changes requested and how did the manager handle it?
- If you were in the shoes of the IT project manager, how would you have handled the change management differently for this project?

References

Cavalcanti, Y.C., do Carmo Machado, I., Neto, P.A.D.M.S., & de Almeida, E.S. (2016). Towards semi-automated assignment of software change requests. *Journal of Systems and Software*, 115, 82–101.

Portny, S.E. (2011). *Project Management for Dummies*. New Jersey: John Wiley & Sons.

Chapter 4

"Do You Have Enough Data?" Planning Phase Blunder at Diva Hospital

Abdullah El Nokiti
British University of Dubai

Aditi Mishra
Careem

Khawla Mubarak
Emirates Airlines

Contents

4.1 Introduction

Mr Tony is the manager of a project titled "Time: The Efficient Solution to Monitoring Operating Room Timing Events." The aim of the new system is to measure the main steps that are followed in every operating room at the main branches of the hospital. The aim of the project is to identify and investigate the main reasons for delaying operations at the time that they have been scheduled to begin.

The system is designed to synchronise with the hospital's aim to improve and develop its current processes. Operating rooms are critical environments that require special conditions. Once the system is used effectively, it will facilitate the punctual execution of planned operations, thereby resulting in shorter wait times and the better use of resources.

For the hospital's new chief medical officer (CMO), Mr Tarek, unnecessary delays in the operating room are unacceptable; he, therefore, wanted to identify the reasons for the delays and help to eliminate them. The total number of daily delays per operating room can be combined to schedule an extra operation; consequently, this project is one of the new CMO's top priorities.

4.2 Organisational Background

Established in 1985 in the UAE, Diva Hospital is dedicated to providing state-of-the-art medical services to the public. Under the instruction of H.H. Sheikh Mohammed Bin Butti and Dr Kassem Alom, the hospital was established in Abu Dhabi and has a fast-growing network of hospitals throughout the country. Taking into consideration the quality of care and safety of all patients, Diva Hospital partnered with ISO, as well as the world leader in healthcare certification—the Joint International Commission—to ensure that the latest quality conformance standards are being met.

Growing from a small polyclinic into a major health services provider with 3 main hospitals and 17 medical centres, Diva Hospital continues to strive for excellence and innovation as its basic standard. Adding to this, since its establishment approximately 30 years ago, Diva Hospital has succeeded in introducing the following services:

- Laparoscopic surgery
- IVF services
- Open surgery

- Nephritic chemical analysis
- Cosmetic surgery

In addition, Diva Hospital currently offers the following services:

- Medical services
- Surgical services: orthopaedics; ear, nose, and throat; ophthalmology; urology; neurology; cardiology; bariatrics (weight loss); plastic and cosmetics; and paediatrics
- Critical care unit: intensive care unit, cardiac care unit, neonatal intensive care unit, emergency services, and anaesthesia
- Internal medicine
- Cardiology and cath lab
- Dermatology and cosmetology
- General medicine
- Dentistry
- Oncology
- Nephrology
- Neurology
- Nuclear medicine
- Psychiatry and psychology
- Physical medicine and rehabilitation
- Diagnostic and other services: radiology, laboratory, pharmacy, and nutrition and health education

Diva Hospital decided on the following main strategic plan:

- Vision: To provide the highest-quality medical care to patients while taking medical excellence into consideration. Passion, commitment, and the highest health standards are the main deliverables.
- Mission
  - To be the first choice for patients by building a very good reputation
  - To be patient centred by applying the most recent trends in the healthcare world
  - To apply the highest safety and quality standards while providing a pleasant environment
  - To ensure the effectiveness and efficiency of the practical methods used to train employees

- To ensure that staff provide services which are aligned with the hospital's values
- To evaluate the needs of the market and continuously deploy the best practices and technologies
- To be pioneers in the health industry and create partnerships with international medical organisations
- To support the deployment of IT to facilitate the hospital's achievement of its main objectives

■ Values
- Integrity
- Innovation
- Collaboration
- Accountability
- Results
- Excellence

Another important factor that can have a positive effect on organisational success is the ethical management of staff. Diva Hospital has an ethics framework in place, as well as a committee that is dedicated to ensuring that strong ethical practices are followed by the organisation. This framework is used to define the organisation's role, the expectations of its stakeholders, and the operation of business at a high moral level (Figure 4.1).

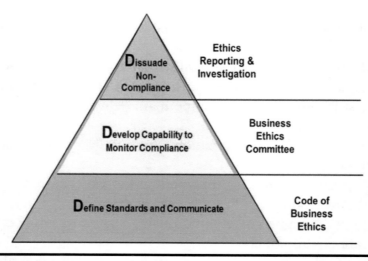

Figure 4.1   Ethics framework at Diva Hospital.

The figure above shows the expected actions to be taken once an ethical dilemma arises:

1. Standards definition is managed in keeping with the hospital's code of ethics document.
2. The main role of the Business Ethics Committee is to develop ethics capabilities and monitor the level of ethics.
3. Immediately after detecting an issue, which does not coincide with the Code of Ethics document, it should be reported and investigated.

Diva Hospital wanted to provide better services to its patients; therefore, it was important to deploy experts who have previous experiences and who are able to drive the organisation towards success. The chart below shows the main members of the new C-level management (Figure 4.2):

Mr Tony recapped the beginning of project development by stating, "We used to have tailored software designed only for the hospital, but the language was old." The hospital's management discussed whether to purchase an health information system (HIS) or develop one internally. This was a challenge for Mr Tony, considering how small his team was.

The growth of the system continued, with more branches being added later on, as well as an increased number of employees—over 600 physicians and 900 nurses. As a result of this, the hospital's management wanted to shift from decentralised branches to one HQ that was linked to all other branches. This important change represented an excellent opportunity for the hospital, as the demand for health insurance had increased significantly between 2001 and 2013, heralding a new age of medical services.

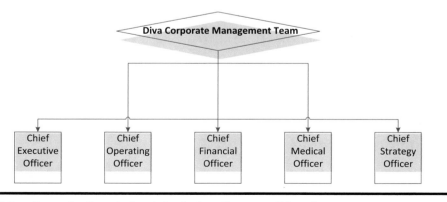

Figure 4.2   Organisational chart depicting the new C-level management.

This "bombing" effect required Mr Tony's team to work harder and adopt the latest technologies that were available on the market. With the introduction of the HQ, and the aim of converting to a centralised method of management, the new C-level management wanted to improve the hospital's services and deliverables.

4.3 Case Description

As with any other organisation, it was important for Diva Hospital to continue to expand its IT systems. Considering the fast-changing environment and legacy systems, the organisation's new CMO wanted to implement a change to enable the hospital to improve its services and compete more effectively against its competitors.

It was reported to the CMO that the procedures taking place in the operating rooms were repeatedly delayed and were being performed poorly.

"We used to schedule five operations, but only three would be completed. There were many time gaps that may have allowed for additional operations, and this cost us money & effort," Mr Tony explained. Furthermore, he stated, this was common to all the branches.

Mr Tarek knew that solving minor problems was often the key to major success. He involved Mr Tony and his new team in his efforts to resolve the issue. After conducting several brainstorming sessions, the IT team decided on and began to implement a solution.

"The new system was simple, innovative and smart," explained Mr Tony.

The idea was a set of steps in a certain workflow. A big button in the middle was used to trigger the end of the current step and begin the subsequent one. As confirmed by the CMO, an operation involves 12 main steps. By the end of the last step (in the case of a delay), the system suggests and shows predefined reasons for the delay. These data are later used to enable more accurate timing that is used to help set appointments for both patients and staff.

4.3.1 The Road Map to the Project

Mr Tony and his team knew that one key to the success of such a project was to ensure that all team members, including the hospital staff, had a common understanding of how the new system would be implemented and used.

"We spent quite a long time on brainstorming sessions to find the closest point in which the system would best serve the operations room," said Mr Tony.

He wanted to implement a state-of-the-art type of project that would be used as a benchmark in the region. Project Management Professional (PMP) guidelines were used to decide on and plan the project phases. Top management awaited the project charter, which was formulated according to the requirements, while defining the main stakeholders who would benefit from the system. A mock-up implementation was also demonstrated to them. Finally, Mr Tony received approval to start the project as soon as the agreement was signed.

At this stage, Mr Tony knew that he was carrying quite a heavy load on behalf of the IT department. He wanted to ensure delivery of the system while adhering to the approved budget and schedule. As with any other project, sudden changes may occur, and only a good project manager is able to adapt to such changes while minimising losses. During the development stage, our quality assurance team stated that only medical-grade hardware is approved to enter the operating room. This is because such devices should be checked regularly because they are being used in a critical environment. Moreover, the new device should have the following specifications:

- It should be an all-in-one machine for ease of use
- It should support Windows operating systems
- It should be able to be connected to the hospital's main website domain

Considering these new requirements, which had not been communicated earlier, the IT team immediately began to look for a new vendor who would be able to supply such a device. Meanwhile, Mr Tony arranged for his team members to visit the operating room to enable them to familiarise themselves with the environment and confirm how the new device would be installed, as operating rooms typically have numerous pipes, and drilling is allowed in only certain places. Moreover, whenever the team members wanted to visit an operating room to run a mock test or conduct trepanning for the end user, they needed to ensure that there were no operations being undertaken, and they needed to follow a strict cleaning process before entering the room.

An international vendor specialising in the aforementioned requirements was eventually selected. However, this was not a complete relief for the team, as the cost of the new device was ten times the amount that had been allocated in the planned budget, and the estimated shipping period was 2 months longer than expected. Such changes would require the approval of top management.

"I do remember that our management was so supportive and encouraging. They approved the new budget and accepted the delay in project delivery. As a result, we needed to amend the PM plan to match the new updates," explained Mr Tony.

4.3.2 Weak Acceptance Level

Finally, the test hardware unit arrived, and the software itself was developed and tested. Mr Tony and his team installed the unit after receiving the approval of the QA team. It was now time to step back and begin monitoring the results. The data monitor coordinator noticed that after the implementation of the new system, only new transactions were being generated. Mr Tony recapped what had happened during the project, stating,

> If I had the ability to go back in time, to the initial period of the project, I would make the following changes. As the project manager, I'd have performed on an interactive basis, not a reactive one. Fixability is a key factor, and it would have helped in case of any change request. Enhancements could also have been performed from day one of the project.

Considering the fact that this project was conducted in such a critical environment, Mr Tony was thankful for the support of senior management, who provided him with extra time and money. Nonetheless, one of the main reasons why the project failed was the stakeholders' high resistance to change.

4.4 Solutions and Recommendations

The following are some of the solutions and recommendations that would help to support and improve the case study above:

■ The importance of identifying the scope of the project: In this chapter, a study was conducted between the identification of a more accurate scope and the final performance or delivery of the outcomes. Based on the research, it was concluded that a more defined scope would be advantageous in regard to the delivery of a more fruitful project. When applying this knowledge to our case, we found that the CMO did not provide accurate reasons for the delay. This affected the end users, resulting in their inability to use the system. In addition, the new system should have had some level of flexibility to add new reasons for the convenience of the staff (Pretorius & Banda, 2016).

■ Communication is a key element that should be identified: One of the main aspects of the success of any project is how team members communicate with each other. Failure to establish an effective communication plan may lead to the discontinuation of the project. The article outlined the importance of maintaining a suitable communication level, as well as methods of doing so. Linking this to our case, it is evident that the end users did not express their views on the problem as it occurred; they preferred to remain in their comfort zone, which meant not using the system (Mihai & Mihai, 2016).

■ Level of awareness and professional responsibility: In this chapter, a study was conducted on 313 managers at a registered research organisation. The study results showed that each profession should develop a set of ethical standards to be followed, as this would result in employees having greater responsibility with regard to their work. Linking this to our case, some doctors did not want to be tracked, which would show their reasons for delaying the surgeries. The application of ethical standards at work will increase employees' awareness, and as a result, they will begin to use the system in a way that will help them perform their tasks more effectively and efficiently (Valentine & Fleischman, 2008).

■ Project requirements: The final topic showed how helpful and important it is to analyse project data requirements in detail. This analysis was conducted among four teams of different sizes, and the results showed better deliverables of the final version of the software. In this case, the data requirements were a key element, as they caused the delays in delivery and increase in the budget. It is very important for the project team to know from day 1 that only certain approved devices can enter the operating room. However, because the Quality Office did not mention this, the project was delayed, and plans needed to be changed (Ziółkowski, Orłowski, & Wysocki, 2013).

4.5 Lesson Learned Questions

- How did the project team overcome the problem of the poor data requirements analysis?
- How did poor data requirement collection affect the project?
- What is the reason for poor data requirement collection?

References

Mihai, C. & Mihai, R. (2016). Communication management and team working sale. *Valahian Journal of Economic Studies*, 7(3), 9196.

Pretorius, L. & Banda, R.K. Jr. (2016). The effect of scope definition on infrastructure projects: a case in Malawi's public and private implementing agencies. *The South African Journal of Industrial Engineering*, 27, 203–214.

Valentine, S. & Fleischman, G. (2008). Professional ethical standards, corporate social responsibility, and the perceived role of ethics and social responsibility. *Journal of Business Ethics*, 82(3), 657–666.

Ziółkowski, A., Orłowski, C., & Wysocki, W. (2013). Knowledge management in the processes of project requirements analysis. *Studia I Materialy Polskiego Stowarzyszenia Zarzadzania Wiedza / Studies & Proceedings Polish Association for Knowledge Management*, 65, 106–120.

Chapter 5

Multicultural Issues and Problems at Nayah Transformation Planning Construction Project

Chandni Joshi
Chronometer General Trading

Kanika Gambhir
Silicus Technologies

Pranav Patil
StarLink

Shweta Rajderkar
Leap Development

Contents

5.1 Introduction

"Good morning, Mr Faraz!" said Sundaram, one of the Nayah Transformation Planning (NTP) construction team members, who was working on a project related to the post-tensioning system used in high-rise buildings.

Sundaram was always the first employee to arrive at work. He spoke little English but always started his day at the construction site with a smile. Ahmad Faraz, the construction manager of a high-rise five-star hotel, returned the greeting. Mr Faraz wanted to do outstanding work on the hotel building, as it was his first project in Dubai. Before coming to Dubai, he had worked in Egypt for 5 years and received a great deal of appreciation and numerous awards for his outstanding contributions to construction projects. However, he had no experience working with a culturally diverse team. This was going to be his first time handling a team whose members were from different parts of the world. As Dubai is a land of attractive high-rise buildings, Mr Faraz was excited to start working. The project was special to him because it was the first high-rise construction that he had been appointed to oversee.

Mohammad Zoidee, CEO of the company, gathered the team members for a meeting that morning. Looking at the faces of all the construction workers and engineers, he said,

> Good morning, everyone! As many of you know, Mr Faraz has been appointed the new manager for this project. We have completed many projects to date, but this one is going to be different and interesting, as Mr Faraz will be leading the team. This is one of our biggest projects, and I am expecting all of you to co-ordinate with Mr Faraz and impress me with great work. All of you come from different parts of the world and contribute to our work here. I expect each one of you to be honest in regard to both your work and your co-workers. If you have any issues, you can always count on Mr Faraz for help. All the best, guys!

Mr Faraz then said with a smile, "Let's get to work," after which he immediately left without any further interaction with the team members. All the workers then returned to their assigned jobs.

The construction team was made up of 50 people who came from different geographical and cultural areas. Some of the workers were newly appointed, while some had already been working with the company, but on other projects. The deadline for this high-rise building project had initially been 2 years. But the client had suddenly changed the deadline to one and half years for some reason, and if the NTP did not agree, then the company might as well lose out on the project. The CEO decided to have a quick meeting with the manager and other members of the board of directors regarding this issue. They concluded that even if the schedule was going to be tight, it was better to start working harder instead of losing such a big project and facing financial losses as well.

It was now Mr Faraz's turn to talk to the team and convey this message. He arrived at the site and gathered the workers. He stated, "Change of plans, people! We are gonna have to work extra hours but with the same dedication. The client needs to finish the building within one and half years."

Obvious disappointment spread among the workers and engineers, and they murmured among themselves, "It's just not possible!"

Mr Faraz could see the displeasure on their faces. He motivated them by saying, "If we succeed at this, we will be given great rewards for this achievement . . . maybe some cash, too."

Sundaram stepped forward and asked, "What if we fail"?

"Let's just say that failure is not an option here," Mr Faraz replied.

Because of their disappointment, the team members initially came together. But as the days went on, they started noticing the differences among them. They had different communication styles, their working styles were differ-ent, their ways of looking at the managers and following their orders were different, and they had different beliefs and cultures. All of these differ-ences eventually started coming between the workers and creating problems amongst them. Frequent fights started to happen, and the workers' use of abusive words increased. The miscommunication among them started to affect their work. The project was already going to fall behind schedule, and now, because of these issues related to their multicultural backgrounds, the work started lagging even more.

One day on site, while everyone was working, one of the workers said something abusive to another because he did not understand his language. Apparently, a friend of the recipient of the abuse helped him understand what had been said. Eventually, there was a major fight between the two men, and it affected the productivity of the other workers, too. Mr Faraz interfered in the fight and attempted to stop it. But the level of tension remained, and the fights became more frequent; sometimes they were due to language, sometimes due to culture, sometimes due to working styles, and sometimes due to power distance. They were falling way behind schedule because of these frequent fights. Moreover, as previously mentioned, Mr Faraz had no experience handling a multicultural team. He, therefore, started facing many management challenges. He tried to solve the issues by talking to the workers, but it did not help. He was now very worried, because it was important to get the work done within the deadline. But, now, the question was *How?*

5.2 Organisational Background

NTP is an emerging company in Dubai, UAE, that meets ISO 9001:2008 (UKAS) standards. The reason for choosing NTP for this case study is that it is an emerging company in the UAE with more than 200 employees. The construction business in the UAE is always booming. Construction compa-nies contribute significantly to the country's economic development and, therefore, hold a vital position. However, when people from different coun-tries come together for work purposes, conflicts occur. Hence, it is important to study the challenges and possible ways to overcome them in order for the business to succeed. The following section sheds light on the background of the company.

Vision: To provide a service that not only meets but also exceeds our client expectations.

Mission: To build the finest products, develop the business in a way that inspires, and implement solutions to the environmental crisis while benefitting the customers.

These outlined values are the basis of the company's market success (due to building safe, high-quality products) and contribute to an improved world with charismatic and beautiful buildings, which advance the efforts to save it.

NTP is an independent private group, which has its headquarters in Australia, as well as subsidiary companies in UAE, the United Kingdom, and Bulgaria. NTP has become a prominent name in the post-tension field of construction, which also provides value engineering and innovative designs, along with professional services and quality while constructing high-rise buildings, commercial buildings, residential buildings, hotels, and airport developments. It delivers work of the best quality and continues to improve the service that it delivers to customers and clients. NTP's quality assurance policy requires the company to perform a full complement of review systems along with work statements and procedures, which are in place for every phase of the business, including administrative and site operations.

The company's clients admire its commitment for delivering the highest-quality work on time and within the provided budget. The company pays a great deal of attention to health, safety, and the environment. Its main commitment is to build on experience and improve its capabilities and expertise in post-tensioning systems for high-rise buildings and civil engineering structures. Since 1998, the NTP Group has shown tremendous growth in the Middle East in a controlled and professional manner, which has led to the completion of increasingly demanding and complex projects. It has also built a large number of slab projects on multi-storey buildings with different designs in the Middle East.

The company's development is consistent, and the group expects to continue its strong and continuous growth in the market, leading to its expansion all over the world. The current project that NTP has undertaken, which is the subject of this case study, is the construction of a five-star high-rise building in Dubai. The group of people working on the project are from multicultural backgrounds. As we were asked to keep the details confidential, the names used in the case have been changed, and some other details remain undisclosed.

5.2.1 NTP Management

NTP has highly experienced and skilled managers in every sector who are able to co-ordinate and control every facet of the business to achieve profitable results. The company also has qualified structural engineers who are fully experienced in post-tensioning design and who understand structural behaviour and detailing. The following are the holders of key positions within the company:

- Eng. Tim Ways—Partner and Director
- Eng. Amr Yaseen—Area Manager and Head of the Engineering Department
- Eng. Saad Kazali—Managing Partner and Director
- Mohammad Zoidee—CEO
- Mr Ahmed Faraz—Responsible for the current project

5.2.2 Project Details

5.2.2.1 Construction of a High-Rise Five-Star Hotel

Time allotted for construction: 2 years

Highlight: Delay in construction due to multicultural diversity among the workers.

5.2.2.2 Status Diversity

Nationality Identified	Number of Employees
UAE nationals as owner/developer	3
GCC nationals as upper management	40
Americans as management (CM)	10
Iranians/Iraqis as management (CM/GC)	7
Filipinos as technicians	25
Pakistanis, Indians, and Chinese as labourers	100

5.2.3 *The Beginning of the End*

Enshassi and Burgess (1991) found that construction managers working in cross-cultural contexts needed to have a strong awareness of cultural differences and to be able to adapt their managerial styles to enable them to effectively manage multicultural workforces. Rabbat and Harris (1982) studied international construction firms operating in the Middle East and raised the issue of the need for managers to adapt to the local culture to reduce conflict and lessen its implications for project outcomes.

5.3 Case Description

Mr Faraz was sceptical about the workers' ability to complete the project on time. He could never have imagined that working with a multicultural team would have led to so many problems. The following sections address some of the major problems and issues that he faced.

5.3.1 *Status Hierarchy*

"This job was beginning to feel very difficult, since everyone was classified based on their nationality and ethnicity," explained Mr Faraz.

From his observations, the worth of a worker was based on his nationality, and there were numerous cultural stereotypes and prejudices evident among the workers. According to Mr Faraz's observation, it was difficult to figure out why the workers were always at each other's odds. It seemed as if the crew was not operating harmoniously. The reason for one of the major conflicts seemed to have been derived from the hierarchical relationship at work, which collided with the Indian caste system, according to which the worker would have been the supervisor, and vice versa. Hence, these conflicts erupted and led to a great deal of problems, which further affected the project.

5.3.2 *Divergent Norms and Values*

Numerous divergent norms and values seem to exist among employees working on a multicultural construction project. Values describe what is preferred or desired, whereas norms define how something should be done. The different ideas and beliefs of various cultures lead to new challenges and conflicts. The manager faced issues due to the various fights among workers of different nationalities. Most fights occurred due to differences in religious affiliations, while others were caused by differences in opinions.

A safety issue arose when a supervisor asked a worker to jump a seven-foot gap between beams that were over 30 ft above the ground. The worker felt that he had no option because he did not have the right to disagree with a superior, according to the hierarchical system. Even with the presence of the safety officer, the worker felt compelled to follow the dangerous instruction.

The conflicts did not occur solely in the field; they also took place within the offices. The technical and management staff had their fair share of aggressive conflicts as well.

Mr Faraz stated, "My American colleague felt a sense of urgency for every task at hand, whereas my British co-workers had a much more relaxed approach."

This made it more difficult to align the interests of all the parties that were involved.

5.3.3 *Communication Barrier*

Communication has always been a key issue when it comes to multicultural project teams. Mr Faraz found it very difficult to find the correct phrases to motivate everyone to work in harmony and resolve their problems. There were a few pitfalls due to the translation of phrases. NTP recruited 20 new labourers to support its safety staff. The major issue that arose was that none of them spoke English. Mr Faraz, therefore, decided to hire a translator.

The safety engineer stated that "there should be a handrail at 0.5 meters," which was translated as "There should be a handrail."

Hence, these translation errors led to further confusion and delays in the completion of the task at hand. Finding the appropriate phrasing to encourage and motivate workers was challenging; in addition, all of these workers and labourers were from different backgrounds and spoke dozens of different languages, of which only one individual could speak more than one.

In another incident, a huge conflict took place among the Indian and Chinese labourers, who were yelling and screaming at each other as if they were characters in an old war movie. Apparently, a Chinese labour had accidentally dropped a hammer on the Indian labourers. But the language barrier made it difficult for the Indians to understand what the Chinese labourer had to say, which, in turn, led to a huge misunderstanding.

5.3.4 Lack of a Proper Plan

There was no proper planning; everyone simply wanted to see progress occur despite the lack of proper direction.

The client stated, "I want this," without providing a structured plan or instructions.

Unfortunately, because Mr Faraz wanted his first project to be a success, he simply agreed to every demand that the clients had. Most subordinates also simply agreed because they wanted to seem responsive and did not want to risk losing their jobs. Different cultures have different ways of reacting to change. This came between the employees, eventually leading to miscommunication, which, in turn, increased the misunderstandings that arose among them.

5.4 Solutions and Recommendations

To resolve these challenges, Mr Faraz and his team decided to implement the following strategies.

5.4.1 Cultural Awareness

According to Mr Faraz, cultural awareness requires proper attention. He stated, "It is very important to spend time learning about the culture of the local community and to understand the cultures of the various team members."

Staffing a security gate: According to Mr Faraz, if he did not have knowledge of the cultural hierarchies, he would have been unable to staff the security gates.

Approval of new hires: Mr Faraz tried to understand the cultural environment while staffing the project. He stated that without this understanding, the managers would have ended up creating a project estimate that was not acceptable because of the complexity of the government functions in regard to determining what is acceptable and what is not.

5.4.2 Flexibility and Adaptability

Flexibility and adaptability are essential to multicultural mega projects. We live in a world in which the rules of the game keep changing; hence, the capability to adjust to these changing needs is the sole factor determining the success or failure of a project. These needs include government requirements—for example, regarding the use of specific hiring practices and the imposition of mourning periods. In addition, the changing needs in regard to the organisational structure require the employees occupying different roles to easily adapt to changes.

5.4.3 Development and Building of Relationships

Relationships are the most important factor in project management. It is difficult to build relationships but easy for them to break down. If relationships are properly maintained, conflicts can be avoided, and numerous challenges can be resolved.

5.4.4 Neutral Third Party

Having a neutral third party can help to resolve the various conflicts that arise, provided that all the project members respect this party, which is generally called a safety team. Regarding the case in which one of the workers dropped a hammer, the safety team played an important role. The safety team helped to resolve the conflict between the two workers because the team members knew the languages that both men spoke.

5.4.5 Cultural Matching

Based on this strategy, the construction manager matches the employees with others who have similar cultural backgrounds and languages, as this decreases the challenges of cross-cultural communication. Mr Faraz stated,

> When I see that I need to talk to a contractor whom I cannot really communicate with . . . I can have another person who I think can better relate to them deal with them. And that, I am finding, is very useful.

Therefore, to resolve the issue with a subcontractor, Mr Faraz paired the contractor with another team member who had a similar cultural background.

After looking at the challenges and strategies that were identified in this case, we came up with some recommendations to overcome the issues that arose. These are outlined below.

5.4.6 Documentation of Lessons Learned and Successful Strategies

It is crucial to document the lessons learned and strategies incorporated to prevent and resolve the issues that arise in a project. If the issues are not documented, the team will keep pursuing the same course of action and end up having to resolve same kinds of issues repeatedly. The challenges that were referred to in this case were issues that could have been easily resolved by taking certain steps at the beginning of the project.

5.4.7 Execution of Team-Building Activities before Beginning Operations

One of the team members working on the project stated, "We had lots of conflicts among ourselves." For example, the team members were from various backgrounds and had different views about being on time. In addition, the Americans, for instance, had a style that involved aggressively pushing the project. Therefore, if all the team members learned about each other's cultures, this increased the understanding among them. Thus, at the start of the project, team-building activities must be included, as this helps to reduce the conflict among project members (Furber, Smith, & Crapper, 2012).

5.4.8 Programme-Specific Incentives

In this case, there was intense competition among the construction managers. Even though all the managers were interested in the success of the project, they were more focused on their individual success. Hence, incentives can be used to encourage the employees to work as a team, which will improve the relationships between the team members and will result in the success of the project.

5.4.9 Inclusion of a Bilingual Individual

In addition to the safety team, the construction manager should have a multilingual individual who works at all the locations and who coordinates with all the crew members. This multilingual individual will play an important role in resolving conflicts.

5.5 Lesson Learned Questions

- What do you think are the issues related to cultural diversity in a construction project in NTP?
- What approaches or strategies do you recommend for the manager to overcome these issues so that the work is done smoothly and faster? Discuss the solution for the problems identified.
- What are the main reasons for having clashes at the workplace in a multicultural team? Discuss root cause of issues in cultural diversity.

References

Enshassi, A. & Burgess, R. (1991). Managerial effectiveness and the style of management in the Middle East: an empirical analysis. *Journal of Construction Management and Economics*, 9(1), 79–92.

Furber, A., Smith, S. & Crapper, M. (2012). A case study of the impact of cultural differences during a construction project in Ghana. In S. Smith (ed.), *Proceedings of the ARCOM 28th Annual Conference*. ARCOM, pp. 553–562, 28th Annual ARCOM Conference, Edinburgh, UK, 3–5 September.

Rabbat, O. & Harris, R.B. (1982). Managing employee conflict in the Middle East. *Journal of the Construction Division, ASCE*, 108, 219–225.

Chapter 6

Planning, Culture, and Technology Management Disruption at Al Muqarrabah Paramount Company

Muhammad Faizzan Zafar
Emmar

Abdullah Siddiq
Ajman University

Jean Edmond El Kesserwani
CG Technology LLC

Bilkisu Aminu Suleiman
Hamon Cooling Tower Company

Contents

6.1 Introduction

For the past 10 years, Mark Hinds has worked as a senior consultant at Al Muqarrabah Paramount Company (AMPC). For him, reaching this position in the company was difficult. He worked at a construction company before joining this organisation. He is an expert at dealing with customers when it comes to securing contracts. We, as a group at Al Muqarrabah Paramount, interviewed him regarding his project, which ended up being a failure for the organisation. The project was related to his visit to China, where he went to meet a low-level manager of ChingYong Ltd. The basic purpose of his visit was to identify suitable options regarding a hydroelectric project in China and discuss these with the management of ChingYong Ltd. This was Mark's first effort at launching a project internationally. Al Muqarrabah Paramount was contacted by ChingYong Ltd., who was asked to provide the facilities and a design for its hydroelectric plant.

Before his trip, Mark was assured that he would be taking three important devices with him: a laptop, a Surface Pro tablet, and a smartphone. Now, the important thing, he told us, was that these devices had been issued by the company and that he had to use them during his meetings and presentations with ChingYong Ltd. Above all, he explained that he was very conscious about using technology during his presentations, stating that he preferred to write notes during meetings instead of using tablets, laptops, and other forms of technology. The easiest option for him was to carry his briefcase, which contained the documents that he enjoyed writing during every meeting and presentation. He was annoyed by the use of technology, which he said usually made it impossible for him to watch movies on the tablet. He also said that this happened to him while he was travelling to China for his meeting with the ChingYong management. This case study is important for three main reasons: (1) lack of planning, (2) the importance of cultural understanding, and (3) the impact of technology on business.

6.1.1 Lack of Planning

Mark Hinds was informed merely 4 days before his departure date that he would be visiting China to discuss this hydroelectric project. He had no official meetings and was given no instructions in relation to his visit. The basic reason for this was that the organisation had trust in him because his record of dealing with customers was very good, and he had secured numerous contracts for his company, albeit in the local market. Mark was merely informed that he had to take three important items with him on the trip and they would be provided by the organisation. These three items were a laptop, a mobile phone, and a Surface Pro tablet. He was also told that these accessories were connected to the organisation's network.

6.1.2 Importance of Cultural Understanding

As a consultant, Mark Hinds was mature but he had not done any dealing on an international level; consequently, he was lacking with regard to his cultural knowledge of China. He told us that "it was very difficult to understand that what they were expressing concurrent to what they actually wanted. Most of the time, they were poker-faced, and it was very difficult for me to handle the situation." This problem clearly illustrates that the organisation had not focused on the cultural aspect before sending Mark Hinds to China.

6.1.3 Impact of Technology

This is the most important of all the factors related to this case study. In today's era of globalisation and IT, it is important for managers and consultants to have technological know-how. Business is done through different communication media, and network connectivity is one such medium. Business–IT alignment is a key factor in success. However, Mark Hinds was not pleased about having to use these IT resources. He, therefore, faced numerous problems during his visit to China, which eventually resulted in a major loss for the organisation.

6.2 Organisational Background

Al Muqarrabah Paramount Company is located in the western region of Abu Dhabi, near to Al Sila. The central plant was initially constructed in 1993 to help the government's power sector, and the plant began production in 1995–1996. The main goal of the company is to provide power and water facilities to its customers. This goal is dependent on further objectives that are related to efficiency, effectiveness, quality assurance, and the minimisation of overall maintenance and operations costs. One of the main goals of the organisation is to train staff in ongoing innovations to maintain productivity. The company is also focused on saving the environment from production hazards and, more specifically, enhancing the safety of production plant. The organisation is dependent on its administrative, technical, and financial departments. The management consists of the managing director and deputy director, and there are other supporting sections related to IT, inspection, the chemical laboratory, and other areas. Operations are performed by the organisation's staff, who work different shifts and whose work is overseen by their supervisors in their respective departments. Budgets are prepared by the finance department, which helps in different areas, including the purchasing of different kinds of goods.

Al Muqarrabah Paramount Company is keen to implement a health, safety, and environmental management system within the organisation. It is implementing this system in an effort to help secure the environment, which directly affects the health of the people living in the surrounding communities. The aim of the company is to continuously improve the health, safety, and environmental system in accordance with company, federation, and international laws and regulations. For this purpose, the company has defined core elements and processed those that are required for it to meet this particular objective. This objective is related to the ability to understand its environmental implications, and performance is measured against the organisation's clear environmental targets. Other objectives are to minimise the number of incidents and complaints that are related to the environment and to maintain an effective environmental management system.

In 1999, Madinat Zayed Power Plant merged with Al Muqarrabah Central Power Plant, forming a joint venture. The aim was to increase power generation through effective management as a joint corporation. A total of more than 200MWs is generated by both plants, which produce energy to their maximum capacity.

6.3 Case Description

Mark Hinds's flight to Beijing was on time, and the journey was smooth. When he landed at the airport, he was asked by a customs officer whether he was there for business or merely for pleasure.

Mark replied, "I am here on behalf of Al Muqarrabah Paramount Company, and I am here for work."

As a result of this reply, he was taken to a separate room, where he was left alone. His suitcase, which contained his laptop, mobile phone, and Surface Pro, was taken by two custom officers. They searched and scanned the suitcase for almost 10 min, after which the officers returned to the room in which Mark was sitting and handed his suitcase back to him. Mark told us that at this point, he was completely unaware that he was already in trouble. The previous 10 min had been an attempt to conduct a security breach. His laptop had already been accessed using a hardware key logger, which had been deployed by the Chinese government to search for important information, such as Mark's username and password. At that time, Mark was totally unaware of and completely unprepared for such a situation.

A second security breach occurred when Mark arrived at his hotel. He told us that he was given a Wi-Fi password by the attendant at the hotel's front desk. Using the hotel's Wi-Fi, he logged into his email. This entire process was monitored using software, and his information was intercepted. All information related to Mark's email was now available to hotel employees. Moreover, there were more breaches to come.

The third security breach occurred as Mark sat in a restaurant, where he used his mobile phone to connect to the public Wi-Fi. He told us that while he was out for dinner, someone attempted to use his laptop and Surface Pro, which were in his hotel room. When he returned to his room, he noticed that his laptop and Surface Pro had been left open, and both had been left on bed. Therefore, the most serious security breach had occurred even before his negotiations with ChingYong management. It had occurred when he had used the hotel Wi-Fi to prepare his documents and presentations. He told us that he did not know that the government of China had been observing him so closely.

The fourth and final breach took place during his deal negotiations at ChingYong. The hardware key logger that had been installed by the customs officer at the airport was removed while he was at ChingYong, and data were extracted by the company IT employees. In doing so, the laptop was damaged.

During this entire situation Mark knew nothing. He told us that his laptop and even his Surface Pro simply stopped working while he was on his flight back to the UAE. Upon his return, he went to his company's IT section to complain about his laptop and Surface Pro. The IT administrator asked him when his laptop had stopped working. He replied that it had started after his meeting with ChingYong management. He told us that the IT administrator asked him a few more questions, including whether he had been separated from the laptop at any point. Mark replied that the laptop had been taken from him for 10 min at the airport in China. The IT administrator asked Mark whether he used Wi-Fi anywhere, and Mark replied in the affirmative. Mark told us that he narrated his entire trip to the security manager, who arrived at the conclusion described above. The IT administrator told Mark that his laptop had been hacked and that security breaches had occurred five times.

The other problem that Mark told us about was the cultural difference he faced during his negotiations with ChingYong management. Firstly, they wanted to sign a contract agreeing on an affordable amount. Secondly, during his presentation, they were asking for a considerable amount of information; however, their replies contained comparatively information. He told us that "they had blank expressions while I was presenting in front of them. My points were straightforward and focused, but they were looking for more assurances and data. For their part, I felt that they were reluctant to answer my questions and were not being straightforward." Moreover, he told us that "it was the lower management which was dealing with me. I was quite surprised that their middle management or higher management were not involved in such an important deal. And the people sitting there were giving fake smiles at times, though most of the time, they were expressionless. I was confused about whether they were agreeing or disagreeing with my arguments."

In this case study, the first major problem related to planning. Mark's organisation did not work on a negotiation plan, and as a result, he faced numerous problems in China. The second important factor related to the fact in selecting this individual, Al Muqarrabah Paramount Company made the wrong choice. Mark was not good at using technology, which should have been taken into consideration in light of today's era of network connectivity. The problems that he faced were severe as a result of his ignorance regarding the use of technology and the fact that he was unfamiliar with security breaches. The third problem related to cultural diversity. Mark was facing unfamiliar people in an unfamiliar culture, and this meant that he was, at times, placed in an awkward position. The combination of all these problems worked in favour of ChingYong but resulted in a loss for Al Muqarrabah Paramount Company. The contract that was signed was worth US$500 million, which amounted to US$30 million less than the estimate that had been given to Mark Hinds. The project was now a challenge for the organisation, as it was difficult to carry out construction without exceeding the amount that had been agreed to in the contract.

6.4 Solutions and Recommendations

The challenge was to manage this project that Mark signed off and which was $30 million less than the original estimate. This was a result of the compromise that Mark made during his negotiations with ChingYong Ltd. In this section, we will offer solutions to help Al Muqarrabah Paramount Company to successfully complete this project within the agreed-upon parameters. We will also offer recommendations to help deal with such problems in the future. We will recommend steps that were not taken by Al Muqarrabah Paramount, resulting in its unsuccessful negotiations with the Chinese company.

6.4.1 Time Management

The one area that was not included in the signed contract related to the amount of time that the project would take to complete. Al Muqarrabah Paramount could have bought some extra time from its customer, thereby helping the company to use fewer resources to complete the project. The fewer resources used by the company, the less it would have had to pay the employees, and this would have helped save the budget, which was the company's ultimate goal. Time itself is the most important resource, as it plays the key role in defining the success criteria for any kind of project. Time management contains six processes, of which the two most important are activity resource estimation and activity duration estimation. These processes defined the success factor for the Al Muqarrabah Paramount Company's project. The company can take leverage by developing a schedule that enables it to buy extra time from ChingYong and reduce the number of resources used, thereby helping it to adhere to its budget.

6.4.2 Cost Control

Cost control is another important area that an organisation can focus on to enable it to complete a project successfully. This area falls under the monitoring and control process group. This process facilitates the management of changes in the cost baseline and allows for the effective monitoring of the project's status. The cost control inputs include the project management plan, work performance indicators, and organisational process assets. The project management plan also includes the cost baseline, cost management plan, and project-funding requirements. Work performance indicators are used to closely monitor the activities that have started and ensure that the costs of these activities are in keeping with the schedule. The tools and techniques used for cost control are earned value management, forecasting, performance reviews, reserve analysis, and project management software. These tools and techniques should be used by the organisation to achieve the desired output, which is related to budget forecasting; document updates, which are related to cost estimates; and project management plan updates.

6.4.3 Communication Process

The other action that the organisation can take is to ensure that the communication process occurring among its various departments is effective. A strong communication plan can help the organisation ensure that there are strong working relationships among its employees, thereby enabling them to perform their tasks more effectively and efficiently. Once there is proper distribution of information, it is likely that tasks will be performed correctly on the first attempt without encountering any problems. The entire communication process can be monitored and controlled through regular performance measurement, which ensures that each person in a position of authority is accountable for his or her work on a regular basis. Next, stakeholder management can play an important role by focusing on the management process, and any budget-related problem can be discussed and addressed with the involvement of all stakeholders.

6.4.4 Organisational Culture

Focusing on organisational culture can be important in regard to the successful completion of a project for which the budget has been estimated incorrectly. If all team members are committed and motivated and they accept the challenge of undertaking the project within the limitations, they can be successful. Receptivity, learning, and motivation matter, and these are all driven by leadership. Quality leadership can have such a positive impact that the employees are able to produce excellent results. These factors lead to the development of a sense of ownership and dedication among the employees, which, in turn, motivates them to focus more on the project. The employees will feel that the success of the project is their own success. Consequently, organisational culture is one important factor in the achievement of the project requirements.

We have outlined possible solutions for Al Muqarrabah Paramount Company concerning the resolution of the budget estimation issue. We will now focus on what could have been done to avoid the situation in which the company currently finds itself.

6.4.5 Negotiation Process

Negotiation is a five-stage process. Of these stages, the most important is the preparation phase. In the preparation phase, a representative of the company develops the profile of one's counterpart and figures out what the likely demands of the other side will be, the number of possible team members in their group, and their authority with regard to negotiations. The second stage is the relationship building that occurs at the time of the negotiations, which enables the individual to feel confident if he or she is well prepared. The third stage is the exchange of task-related information. The more formal setup begins during this stage. The fourth stage is related to persuasion, which tends to involve underhanded tricks and non-verbal cues about the deal. During the fifth and final stage of the negotiation process, the parties grant concessions to each other and then move towards a conclusion. The entire negotiation process is linked to cultural understanding. This second important issue of cultural understanding was one that did not favour Al Muqarrabah Paramount Company vis-à-vis the Chinese.

6.4.6 Cultural Understanding

Mark Hinds was completely unaware of the Chinese culture and was confused while facing the other side during the negotiations. Firstly, he was not well prepared for the negotiations from a multicultural perspective. In the Chinese culture, the so-called poker faces are the norm; the Chinese will wear a fake smile that does not reflect what they are experiencing on the inside. Secondly, they have comparatively less authority during negotiations, because the power lies with the Chinese government. In other words, negotiators in China have minimal authority to make decisions. Thirdly, in the Chinese culture, efforts are made to speak less and listen more. Consequently, at the time when Mark was presenting, the Chinese were requesting more information, but he reached the point when there was no more information to present.

These cultural differences are important when making international deals or conducting negotiations. In today's world of competition, in which there is no room for error, understanding cultural differences is critical. The next and most important factor was Mark's lack of technological know-how, because of which he lost $30 million when he signed the contract. Business–IT alignment is the most critical factor in the world of network connectivity, as it affects decision-making, strategies, and the implementation of strategies and relationship mechanisms. The company did not select the right individual for the negotiations, as Mark was not careful regarding the use of technology. This could have been due to a lack of awareness, or it may have been due to the culture of the organisation, which placed less focus on the aspect of technological awareness.

6.5 Lesson Learned Questions

- How important is the role of IT in successful negotiations of business deals?
- Are employees of organisation fully aware of technological impact in today's world?
- How to develop an organisational culture in multinational organisations?

Bibliography

Butler, J.B. and Raiborn, C. (2015). Fraud: An ounce of prevention. Cost Management.

Chin, L.S. and Abdul Hamid, A.R. (2015). The practice of time management on construction project. *Procedia Engineering*, 125, 32–39.

Project Management Institute (2013). *Guide to the Project Management Body of Knowledge (PMBOK®)*. 5th edition, Project Management Institute, Washington, DC.

Turner, J.R. (2009). *The Handbook of Project Based Management: Leading Strategic Change in Organization*, 3rd edition, Mc-Graw Hill, New York.

Chapter 7

Implementing Enterprise Resource Planning Project at Al Sidek Hospitals

M. Abdulwadood Marashi
3M

Kimmy Hanspal
Market-i

Sameer Malik Shaik
Emirates Global Aluminium

Zakareya Alalawi
Social Care and Minors Affairs Foundation

Contents

7.1 Introduction

> My most recent position was at UPMC in Italy. UPMC is the
> University of Pittsburgh Medical Center, which manages an
> end-stage organ transplant unit.
>
> **Wissam**

Wissam Ismail joined UPMC 6 months ago as the CIO, prior to which he
worked for Al Sidek Hospitals Group in Abu Dhabi, UAE, as the Group
Director of Information and Communication Technology. During his 7
years at Al Sidek, Wissam was involved with numerous projects, including
the SAP enterprise resource planning (ERP), electronic medical records
ancillary systems and upgrades, pharmacy benefit management, centralised IP telephony, and application life cycle management. Immediately after
he began working at Al Sidek, Wissam realised that he would face a major
challenge in his position, because of legacy systems, decentralisation, and
outdated technology.

Before working at Al Sidek, he was employed to the Roads and Transport
Authority (RTA) in Dubai, where he did extensive work on the Salik project
(Dubai toll system), including on the user interface, system upgrades, and
scratch cards. He came to RTA from TransCore, the main contractor of the
Salik project in Dubai, where he worked as an IT manager and played a
major role in that project. While there, Wissam had done some civil work
and had dealt with the contact centre and data centre. In addition, he had
been exposed to a variety of new technologies and managed a large team,
which was responsible for ensuring the success of the project.

Prior to his arrival in Dubai, Wissam spent numerous years working in
the United States in the IT field. He used to be responsible for the points of
sale for different clients, including gas companies, petrol stations, and other
businesses that required payment transactions.

7.2 Organisational Background

Al Sidek Hospitals Group was established in Abu Dhabi as a polyclinic
30 years ago. Today, the group consists of three large hospitals, two of which
are located in Abu Dhabi and one in Al Ain, as well as polyclinics and a
number of pharmacies. With approximately 4,000 employees, including

600 physicians and 900 nurses, the group provides all types of healthcare services. Until 2010, each branch and facility worked in isolation from others (from an IT/IS point of view). At that time, the group was growing and had a plan to do an initial public offering (IPO), based on the realisation that with its current decentralised infrastructure and asynchronous systems, it would be unable to progress into the future. Most of the software that the group was using had been developed in-house, including its health information system (HIS), ERP, and various other small applications and utilities.

These software applications and systems were maintained by a small team of software developers and had been developed using outdated programming language (Visual Basic 6.0) and software development methodology. As a result of its need to do an IPO, the group had to acquire and adopt new systems and standard technologies. During the period between 2010 and 2016, the group made significant changes by implementing new systems and managing vital IT projects. These changes began in 2010, when the group began putting together a bigger software team to meet the huge business demands, especially with regard to the health insurance mandate in Abu Dhabi. The software team expanded to approximately 15 employees, including a database administrator and software architect. Even with this increase in team size, the demand for more systems continued to be greater than the team had the capacity to supply.

On 15th February 2016, Al Sidek Hospitals Group PLC was acquired by ClinicStar International Limited, after which the name "Al Sidek" gradually began to change to ClinicStar.

7.3 Case Description: The ERP Project Implementation

The most interesting project, which has its ups and downs, is the ERP project.

Wissam

With the strict regulations of the IPO—such as transparency, governance, accountability, and even the requirement for reports to be formatted in a standard way—as well as the growing internal demand for numerous systems—related, for example, to human capital management, assets management, procurement, and finances—the decision was made to bring all facets together under the umbrella of an ERP system.

Before the go-ahead was given for the project, the biggest issue was the resistance coming from the users of the existing systems, because the implementation of the new systems would expose their incompetence. Some users were happy with the current systems and were averse to change (referred to as change resistance) because they felt that any new applications involving automation could lead to staff reductions or process changes and that they, therefore, needed to undergo more training to be able to use the new systems.

A lot of change management was necessary to sell the project.

Wissam

The starting point was to convince the chairman by carrying out a feasibility study that would explain what would be gained and the value that would be added. This task was assigned to a small committee, whose members were asked to prepare the material and obtain the approval of the CEO. The committee members were the COO, CIO, and CFO.

Once the approval of the CEO was secured, they expanded the committee and established a project-steering committee, which contained all heads of department and which would benefit from the outcomes of the project, including the vendor (at a later stage). Multiple subcommittees were established for each business area that the new system would cover, and their members included management and non-management staff.

Wissam was the key person in charge of the project and was involved in it from the early stages—that is, when the group's top management was still involved in the brainstorming phase. The ERP project was a major one and could, in fact, be considered a programme, because it consisted of numerous sub-projects.

7.3.1 Selection Process

Many companies decide to look internally and come up with the requirements for the statement of need, which is then sold as an request for proposal (RFP). They undertake two actions: A request for interest (RIF) to determine which companies are interested in bidding. Most companies develop an RFP and opt for buying a solution. In Wissam's opinion, this was not only wrong but also proven wrong, because if there was a current system or processes, and then the company sought replacements without re-engineering the processes, the vendor would come on board, which would show a whole new system. Now that the vendor would be in-house, the company would be re-engineering its processes, thereby leading to variations, project delays, and an abundance of other issues. Consequently, when the vendor is on-site, this would mean that time is being dedicated to the implementation of these processes. If the processes are being re-engineered, there will also be no internal agreement with the vendor regarding these processes. This is what happened with this project: These various parties were essentially paying the vendor to simply sit back and watch them arguing about how the process should unfold.

7.3.2 Realistic Time Frame

There were many lessons learned, not only in regard to technical areas but also in relation to business. Business maturity was a key factor. An unrealistic time frame was set by the CFO, who was the project sponsor, and it was driven by both internal and external factors. Again, it was the role of IT and the business itself to find outstanding employees who could support the company's direction and vision. If the sponsor is a dictator, this will have a negative effect on the entire project. The views of the project manager have to align with those of other critical company staff in order for significant progress to be made.

In this case, the company management felt that the project could be completed in 6 months.

Employees often say, "YES! We can do it," forgetting that they all have regular jobs to do.

With regard to the lessons learned, "we have to ensure, through governance, that the business process owners are available," Wissam stated.

7.3.3 Manpower

Ideally, at the start of a project, employees must be taken away from their jobs to enable them to work on the project. It is critical for the company to hire more people for the project. These hires should include additional accountants, warehouse workers, material managers, and human resource staff to fill the gap while employees are involved with this big project. The new hires are needed to do the regular jobs, and the existing people need to engage with the new project, because they have the experience and ability to support it. However, this never happened in this case. Even with the feedback from the vendor that the project could not be completed in 6 months, the CFO (project sponsor) insisted on this time frame.

7.4 Solutions and Recommendations

The project was not completed in 6 months; moreover, the scope that was delivered in 9 months accounted for approximately 20%–30% of the company's actual needs. Consequently, this was a major setback for the project. It was clear that other aspects of the project in regard to business process re-engineering could not be completed. Employees cannot place too much emphasis on it with regard to business process re-engineering, because, at the end of the day, they are purchasing a system from the vendor, and it has already been built in a specific way. Employees need to understand that this is not a minor exercise. It is much easier to "go greenfield." For example, if there is a new implementation with a new company, and the new business is straightforward, they can go live in 6 months. Change management when it comes to employees is not easy. Moreover, even in the design phase of a project, employees should be free to create the design, and then the vendor should go back, do the programming, and then return to obtain approval, such as through user acceptance testing of the design. Therefore, these employees should once again be involved, the system should be built completely and approval obtained, and there should be user acceptance of each phase. There should also be user training after user acceptance of each phase has occurred.

One of the biggest problems with the 6-month time frame for going live was that the vendor wanted to do so on 1st January 2014; however, this is one of the busiest times of the year for the business, and especially for the back office, because in December, it closes the books for the year, and then in January, there is a major increase in business. The company cannot afford for the financial system to be down for a few days or to encounter any issues that might cause it to be down for weeks. In this case, a bad decision was made without taking external factors into consideration.

It was a personal decision.

Wissam

In other words, the decision to go live was made by the project sponsor and not by the committee. Because the go-live date was unrealistic, the project was delayed, and as a consequence, the legacy systems were also affected. The management decided that when the ERP project started, it would be best to halt any new developments or enhancements of the legacy systems; these would be put on hold. When the new system was delivered, and it became evident that it did not meet the company's requirements, they should have delivered some of the requirements using the old system, because they could no longer wait for the new system to be implemented. They thought that they had put every effort into the new project that would have replaced the legacy system within 6 months; however, the implementation was delayed.

These delays resulted in a domino effect, as any delay in any deliverable will cause a delay in subsequent deliverables, and so on. This cost the company a vast amount of money, as the agreement with the vendor for delivery in 6 months remained unfulfilled after more than 2 years.

Wissam mentioned another important lesson that had been learned: "When you start a multi-year project, you have to ensure that your business users—your *key* business users—and stakeholders are committed for the duration of the project."

The company should implement bonuses and signed contracts to ensure that users and stakeholders are committed to seeing the project through to completion.

He explained that in the Patient Accounting module, three directors left and were replaced during the course of the project, and each new director had said, "This is not the right way to do this. I want to change this."

According to Wissam, this caused even more delays and a number of deviations from the original plans.

When there are too many changes in the structure of a project, especially when running an automation system, the system is dependent on live structures. Because it depends on people, if an individual changes sections, the system process will no longer coincide with the people process, thereby requiring the company to dump the system and start all over again. This is a very expensive transaction, especially if it recurs; therefore, it is crucial to ensure that the employees who are present at the start of the project remain with it until the end.

> The continuity of people is critical for each project.
>
> **Wissam**

In the end, although they were able to go live, they were late, as there had been too many changes, stops, and redirections. Wissam mentioned that another very important lesson that was learned from this very long project was the importance of adopting some sort of sprint-type delivery project management. There should be no waterfalls and no blueprints, because the business is a live entity. Even if project members are retained and are able to adhere to the agreed-upon timeline, the evolution of business and the external factors make long projects difficult to manage using traditional methods. It is, therefore, necessary to divide the project into chunks with delivery times of no longer than 3 months each.

In summary, managing long-time big projects (more than a year) is critical and should be managed using modern management tools, such as SCRUM or any agile methodology, this can be done by dividing the project into small chunks that can be managed easily and the deliverable of each will be within short period, this will assure that the involved people will not change, and the processes still the same during each sprint.

7.5 Lesson Learned Questions

- What was the system being implemented in this case study?
- Why was it difficult to implement the system in the organisation?
- What were the initiatives taken by Mr Wissam to ensure the smooth transition from the old to the new system?

Reference

Liberatore, M.J., Pollack-Johnson, B., & Smith, C.A. (2001). Project management in construction: software use and research directions. *Journal of Construction Engineering and Management*, 127(2), 101–107.

Chapter 8

"Who is Responsible on This Task?" Changes in the Project Scope at Elafifi Group

Mohammad Nabil Arif
Magnitt

Bilal Jamshed Butt
Pakistan Railways

Sheeba Sonia
Jumbo Electronics

Mohammad Al Sammach
Dubai Police

Contents

8.1 Introduction

In a brightly lit white room, there was a meeting taking place.

"There's a problem, Ahmed," Anwar stated with his head down.
"What kind of problem?" replied Ahmed.
"The same one. Mr Abdullah has expressed his inability to sign the Project
    Acceptance Criteria [PAC] papers for now," said Anwar.
"We've been in constant contact with them throughout the project, and all
    their requirements have been met," said Ahmed.
"Yeah… in fact, I had a meeting with Mr Abdullah a week ago, and he
    seemed happy with everything we had done so far," said Omar.
"Is Mr Yasir OK with the dashboard?" Jim asked Anwar.
"Oh, yes, he is. In fact, just before stepping into this meeting, I got an
    email with his signed PAC document," Anwar told everyone in the
    meeting.
"Well, at least someone is happy with our work," said Omar.
"It's not about the fact that they were all apprised of our work throughout
    the project; it's that they have changed their requirements at the last
    stage. I think I will have to hold a meeting with Mr Abdullah and
    Mr Hamed," said Ahmed in a worried tone.
"Let's meet up day after tomorrow. I will try to meet up with both VPs
    before then," said Ahmed.

The meeting, which was being held in the IT Department of Elafifi Group of
Companies HQ, ended and everyone stepped out of the room.

8.2 Organisational Background

The Elafifi Group is a KSA-based company that was founded in 1981. Three
companies fall under the Elafifi Group. The organisation started off as Elafifi
Travel and Tourism Company in 1981. Since then, it has been providing
world-class customer service in KSA. Elafifi Travel and Tourism arranges
preferential rates for holiday, educational, nature, and venture tours; voucher
services; car rental; and cruise lines and transportation companies in Saudi
Arabia, the United States, Europe, the Middle East, the Far East, Turkey,
North and South Africa, New Zealand, Australia, and other destinations

around the globe. Due to Elafifi Travel and Tourism Company's renowned reputation, it received an award from the Saudi Supreme Commission for delivering the best service and hospitality in KSA. In 1994, Elafifi Hotels had only one hotel; however, by 2010, this had increased to 11 hotels totalling 2,309 rooms located in Jeddah, Makkah, and Madinah. Elafifi Hotels was the first hotel in the Middle East to be awarded ISO 9001 certification.

The Elafifi Group is proud to be a member of associations and organisations, such as the American Society of Travel Agents and the International Air Transport Association. The aim of these organisations was to ease the Hajj and Umrah journeys for pilgrims and to help demonstrate the hotel's potential to be business partners throughout the hospitality industry. They accomplish this goal by offering travel services and accommodating business programmes from which all sponsors can profit by understanding the Group capabilities.

The vision of the Elafifi Group is to be the most desired business partner in the industry in Saudi Arabia; this achievement will guarantee sponsors' interests and the organisation's prospects.

- We envision an association that aims to be favoured, to be at the helm of the hospitality industry, to show thoughtfulness towards guests, and to be one-step ahead of their expectations. We will display our genuine attention to our consumers by fulfilling their desires. We will pay attention to every minute detail, provide our distinguished expertise, and show concern for every customer.
- We envision a productive organisation with effective operating processes, and whose creators are at a level at which their decisions are invigorated and are open to making positive changes. We foresee an organisation whose clients and sponsors are given appropriate responses that showcase approachability.
- We envision a highly skilled staff foundation, based upon which the employees are encouraged to transform concepts into reality.
- We envision an association in which the public is cared for through rigorous knowledge and skill improvement.
- We envision corporation staff members who are familiar with diverse cultures and various challenges.
- We envision the use of innovative and comprehensible technology that boosts the worth of our consumers and helps them improve the performance of their personnel.

8.3 Case Description

Ahmed is the manager of a project to create an Elafifi management dashboard that will provide high-level performance indicators and business performance for the Elafifi companies. The meeting narrated above was held between Ahmed and his team, which consisted of Omar, who was assigned to gather information regarding the project requirements and communications, and Anwar, who was the project's systems analyst and developer. The project was initiated by the CEO of the Elafifi Group with the aim of providing a dashboard for him, as well as for all three VPs of his companies. This would provide relevant information and data, which they currently had to rely on their department heads to provide. Although some of the data were being handled by the system, they were not being optimally utilised because a different set of legacy systems was being deployed in each group. The CEO wanted a single dashboard for himself and his VPs: Mr Yasir, the head of the travels and tours group; Mr Abdullah, the VP of Hotels; and Mr Hamed, the VP of Haj and Umrah services.

After 2 days, the follow-up meeting was called, and Ahmed, Anwar, and Omar were in attendance.

"Well, at least I have now found out what the problem is. I met Mr Abdullah on the day of our last meeting," Jim said to the attendees. He continued,

> He seemed a little worried himself about the whole thing. He even called in his department heads during our meeting. In short, the problem is that HQ asked the VP for each business to make sure all their respective business heads and business managers are also using to fullest extent the dashboard that we created.

"Ahh! No wonder they have had a change of heart and are not signing the docs," said Omar.

"When the project started, I asked them all to make sure to discuss it with their business heads before we went in for the requirement sessions. But they acted as if they already knew everything," added Omar.

Ahmed then stated,

> I was also not being told about this by the management. This should have been part of the project charter. But after I contacted the project sponsor, Mr Yahya, and informed him that one of the

objectives of having these dashboards was that all the concerned business heads and operations heads should benefit from it. I tried convincing them to start a separate project to incorporate this feature of the dashboard, but Mr Alam, the CIO, said that it shouldn't be treated as a separate project, as the requirements gathered from the VP heads should have been elaborate enough to cover this part as well. On top of that, they wanted us to meet the deadlines of the project with this additional scope.

Alice and Bob who are part of the execution team, looked at each other; they both knew what this meant. They would now have to put in extra work and time just to meet the project deadlines in time for next week.

Jim seemed to understand what was going on in their minds. He went on to say,

Like I said, I have already met with Mr Abdullah and his team, Omar. I have finalised a meeting time for you for today, and I want you to go to Mr Abdullah's and Mr Yasir's office and go through their requirements again. Prepare the requirement gap document listing the requirements we already had and the ones they will highlight now.

Looking towards Anwar, Ahmed stated,

I would like you to check to see if there are other systems that have not been connected with our current dashboard database yet and contact their vendors and ask them to provide us with a script to connect to those systems to get the real-time data, as Mr Abdullah and Mr Yasir might have other legacy systems working in their offices that we might have to connect to get the required data. I don't want us to wait till all the requirement analysis has been redone by Omar and then start this process. We already have much less time, and we will have to initiate all the processes parallel to each other in order to save some time. As the time is short, we will be holding a meeting every morning to make sure we can deliver the project in time.

The meeting ended, and Ahmed was the first to walk out. He was thinking about the documents that needed to be updated and especially those containing the resource and time management plans. He was also thinking about discussing this issue during his monthly meet-up with other project managers. Anwar and Omar were also busy planning in their minds how best to complete the project on time.

In the evening, Jim met up his friends from the project management group and discussed the problem with them, explaining that it had arisen because the project sponsor had changed the scope and that this was, therefore, now directly affecting the cost and putting pressure on the project members to meet the deadline. He explained to his friends that the project had been initiated because higher management was having issues with the lack of insight and information. He also noted that this problem resulted in causing managers to receive weak support in regard to their decision-making processes. He was chosen as a project manager to create a dashboard to enable the management to display all the required information, including the performance of all the companies, in the form of graphs. The project charter had been prepared and initiated by the project sponsor, Mr Yahya, who was also the COO, and all three VPs were to sign project-acceptance documents. He had prepared a team that involved Mr Omar, who was responsible for information gathering and communication and Mr Ahmed, the systems analyst and developer, who was responsible for preparing the dashboard and contacting vendors to deal with the legacy systems.

The requirements were gathered from all three VPs, and they were kept up to date during the development period. During the last meeting between the COO and the VPs, the former asked the latter to ensure that the dashboard facility was also extended to their respective finance, operations, and marketing managers. One VP kept his management team abreast of the developments while the requirements were being gathered; however, the other two did not. Now, the first VP had all the requirements incorporated into the dashboard, including the information that was needed by his managers. In addition, only their logins with their required information needed to be displayed when extending the dashboard facility to the managers. The managers working with the other two VPs did not have their required information inputted into the dashboard; consequently, extensive work was needed to capture the data, link this information with the dashboard database, create their login credentials, and customise the dashboard for each manager.

As the project charter was initiated and sent by the sponsor, without the involvement of the project manager, it failed to disambiguate an important aspect; in other words, it did not capture the main requirement and fulfil the primary objectives that the end users required from the project.

8.4 Solutions and Recommendations

Conceptual planning is tactical, and the issues that are addressed during this phase of a project have a significant effect on its objective, progress, and cost. As such, the associated problems can involve multi-level and multi-stage processes, although the issue is normally from the basics to the details as more thorough information is acknowledged (Hayes, 1999). The following four business factors should be understood: (1) business problem, (2) consumer needs, (3) cost-effective analysis, and (4) the project's fit with the strategic IT plan. An introductory project layout can be done based on these factors, which can be identified as a critical consequence of the layout (McNeil & Hartley, 1986, p. 39):

- Knowledgeable staff members who are invested in the planning process
- A project squad that is fully dedicated to the plan
- An understandable and innovative layout
- Useful communication skills, which are important for handing over information

Consequently, even if the project charter comes from the sponsor, the manager should hold a meeting with the sponsor and all the stakeholders mentioned in the charter. This way, any ambiguities can be ironed out, and a clear view of the project needs, objectives, and contributions to overall IT and business strategies can be obtained. As per Project Management Institute (PMI), the inputs, tools, and techniques used to create a project charter are listed below (Figure 8.1).

It is widely acknowledged that many information system's (ISs) projects fail because they have been designed to satisfy the wrong requirements.

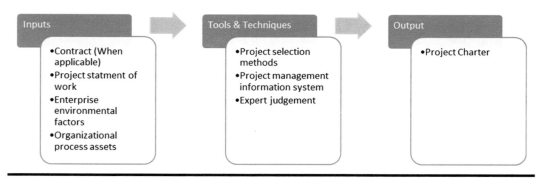

Figure 8.1   Development of project charter (PMBOK, 2013).

Moreover, many projects fail not because they are unworkable but as a result of team members' inability to work the right way. In a changing business environment, in which an organisation's needs and requirements are always changing, this should not come as a surprise. The key objectives of requirement gathering are as follows:

1. Stakeholders should have different stakes in a project to ensure that there is agreement from them all.
2. A basis for software design should be provided.
3. A specific list of outputs should be produced, and deliverables should be tested against these.

As it is common for requirements to be improperly managed, the end user/ business side needs to assume the responsibility of providing clear and prioritised requirements.

The work breakdown structure (WBS) that was created by the project manager was not sufficiently detailed in Figure 8.2 below. The project manager should have sat down with subject matter experts to determine the main project deliverables. Thereafter, they should have divided each deliverable into successively smaller chunks. The WBS has three primary functions:

1. To help integrate the scope of project accurately and specifically.
2. To help assign resources and responsibilities while monitoring and controlling the project.
3. To help double-check all the deliverables with stakeholders to ensure that nothing is missed.

In this case, the WBS was not sufficiently detailed; therefore, there was a failure to perform one of these main functions—that is, to help double-check all the deliverables with the stakeholders.

Although a project charter may be initiated by the sponsor, it should be thoroughly studied and updated by the project manager to ensure that all assumptions and limitations have been properly recorded and approved. A simple miscommunication/ambiguity in the project charter can lead to issues, including project failure. This is what occurred in the above-described case. Moreover, there was an issue with the WBS. A very high-level WBS was created for this project; however, it failed to capture all of its deliverables

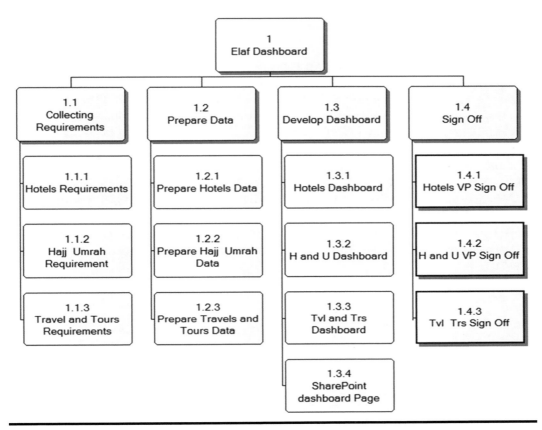

Figure 8.2   Elafifi dashboard project WBS.

and functionalities. Consequently, different dashboard requirements were not mapped with each other, resulting in one stakeholder having his desired requirements fulfilled, while the other two did not. Along with the WBS, if the requirements had been properly mapped and then integrated with each other, the differences between those of similar stakeholders could have been identified and discussed in detail. This might, in turn, have been able to help clarify the ambiguity.

8.5 Lesson Learned Questions

■ What were the problems that led to project issues?
■ Who should have prepared the Project Charter?
■ What processes could have been properly managed to ensure smooth project?

References

Devi, T. R. & Reddy, V. S. (2012), Work breakdown structure of the project, *International Journal of Engineering Research and Applications*, 2(2), 683–686.

Hayes, D. S. (1999), Evaluation and Application of a Project Charter Template to Improve the Project Planning Process. Available at: www.tryonassoc.com/pdffiles/Diane%20Hayes%20Paper.pdf.

McNeil, H. J. & Hartley, K. O. (1986), Project planning and performance, *Project Management Journal*, 17(4), 36–44.

Nikita, N. G., Pujita, K. W. & Sakthi, K. (2012), Managing Requirement Elicitation Issues Using Step-Wise Refinement Model. Available at: https://arxiv.org/ftp/arxiv/papers/1311/1311.1729.pdf.

Project Management Institute (2013), *Guide to the Project Management Body of Knowledge (PMBOK®)*. 5th edition, Project Management Institute, Washington, DC.

Chapter 9

Talaseti Telco Vendor Selection and Process

Basl Ali Zam
Etisalat

Ishtiaq Ahmad
Emirates Airlines

Contents

9.1 Introduction

Ding! Ding!
It was late evening when Andrew answered the phone. "Hello?"
His boss began to yell furiously, "Do you want me to kick you out of the
    company"?
"Nooo … no, sir. I am …" answered Andrew.
"Don't 'sir' me! This is the third time that I have been warned by the
    directors about the late delivery. Why is the Virtual Machine project
    delayed?" blustered the boss.

Andrew replied, "Sir, it's the vendor issue that I have been highlighting for the last 3 months. They have delayed the PDU [power distribution unit], and as a result, there are cascading delays in the RFS [ready for service]."

"Come to my office first thing tomorrow morning!"

With that, dropping his phone with a bang, Andrew's boss ended the call. *Phew!* Andrew thought. *It's not my fault, sir … It's the process.*

Andrew is the project manager for the Engineering section of his company. He has over 10 years of experience in the networking and procurement field. He is technologically savvy, having completed a degree in computer sciences. He then excelled equally in business and obtained an MBA from a local university. He was involved in 3-year long infrastructure-moving projects, during which he dealt with a wide range of vendors and myriad suppliers.

Andrew thinks that vendor selection is the process used by companies to classify, assess, and contract suppliers. It takes a significant amount of company finances to go through the vendor-selection process. In exchange, companies demand high-value products/services from their suppliers. During this process, the companies depend on the prices that are given to them by suppliers, as well as the proposed delivery times and the quality of the materials offered, as these issues are factored into their decision-making. The companies are required to maintain long-term relationships with their suppliers because the vendor-selection process is one of the most important aspects of a firm's operations. This process entails the analysis of suppliers, which should be carried out based on information obtained during previous experiences.

The main issue with the current vendor-selection process at Andrew's company is that it disregards crucial information, focusing solely on financial criteria instead. In this case, end users might only see that the technical requirements have been met within the dedicated budget; however, other requirements, such as service launch date, may be at risk. In this case, Andrew should elaborate the vendor-selection criteria that must be added to the company's vendor-selection process.

9.2 Organisational Background

Talaseti Telco is the leading telecommunications company in the UAE and one of the largest telecommunication companies in the Middle East. Talaseti Telco serves over 11 million customers and over 300,000 enterprise consumers in the UAE, providing a variety of products and services. These include voice services, Internet and data, mobile and network, e-payment, and messaging services. Talaseti Telco operates in 17 countries across Africa and Asia. It was established in 1976 as a joint-stock company. Local governments held a 60% of the company's share, and the remaining 40% was publicly traded.

In 2015, Talaseti Telco reported revenue of 51.7 billion dirhams and a net profit of over 8 billion. Its total market capitalisation is currently 87.7 billion. Talaseti Telco is one of the two telecommunications service providers in the UAE, the other being Du. The company's size, and its data availability and the number of projects that it has conducted, are the main reasons behind the selection of Talaseti Telco for our case study.

9.3 Case Description

Three months ago, during the kickoff meeting about a new computer-expansion project for the cloud, I was discussing the project implementation plan with Mr Mark, the project manager, who represents the vendor with whom the company was dealing. He had just informed me that the vendor had encountered a problem that would prevent the power distribution units (PDUs) from being delivered on time. He indicated that he expected delivery to take another 2 months. The PDUs were supposed to be delivered before any other equipment; this, therefore, meant that the entire configuration process would be delayed.

Because of this interruption, the actual ready for service (RFS) date would be pushed back by 2 months. When Mr Mark was asked to explain the reason for the delay, he claimed that the PDUs that we had requested were not in high demand in the local market, which, in turn, decreased their availability. As a result of our specific requirements, the vendor had been required to order the PDUs from Mexico.

At this point, the issue became confusing, as the purchase order (PO) had been issued 2 months prior, which did not justify the delay. When I asked Mr Mark about the PO once again, he simply said that they could not proceed with the equipment purchase immediately due to the budget issues that his company's Business Department was facing at the time. We attempted to find another solution and even considered a different type of PDU; unfortunately, no other type could work for us, as it is difficult to find one that is compatible with the specs of the hardware that our company was using.

The "New Computer Expansion" project was highly visible. The aim was to deliver virtual machines (VMs) to private customers. This involved internal and external customers or "end users," which was the term that was used to refer to them. Our management and customers would not be pleased about the delay, as the demand for VMs was high, and they had repercussions for financial performance.

Andrew was disappointed with the vendor's performance, especially because it was the third computer-expansion project that his company had signed with this vendor. He called another meeting with my director and other team members to discuss the issue. However, the meeting was not beneficial, as the PO had already been released, and finding another vendor to satisfy our requirements would cost more time. I raised the question of why we had chosen the same vendor despite having had bad experiences with this vendor in the past when it came to the delivery and closing the project in a timely manner.

The response from my manager was simply, "They have lowest price."

The vendor was penalised for the third time for not meeting the contractual RFS date. According to the Contracts Department, a penalty worth 10% of the total PO amount should be imposed as a result of the inability to meet the contractual RFS date. Along with this, the Technology Certificates Department issued the RFS certificate based on the actual RFS date, which was 2 months away from the contractual RFS date. The actual RFS date on the certificate defines the start date of the warranty and support period for the deployed system. The vendor, therefore, had to cover the cost of these 2 months. Additionally, the vendor's performance was rated as "poor" in the final evaluation report, which was submitted to the Contracts Department. However, it seemed as if the vendor's poor performance was not considered; therefore, the imposition of the penalty was the only action that was taken.

One proposed solution to enable the avoidance of delays in the execution phase is to amend the PO to reduce its amount by the price of the PDU. However, amending the PO and issuing another PO will lead to almost the same delay length and extra effort. Therefore, purchasing the PDUs from another vendor was not an option, in this case. I then discussed the delay with the internal end users; however, no justification for the delay was deemed satisfactory. In contrast, showing them the commercial evaluation based on which the vendor was selected improved the situation, as the end users acknowledged the savings that resulted from selecting this vendor.

After floating the request for quotation (RFQ), with the materials that we wanted, the vendors submitted two offers: one financial and the other technical. A committee was then formed to evaluate the vendor's financial and technical offers, based on which an evaluation report would be built, and one vendor would be recommended to the management based on this report. Vendors are evaluated based solely on technical and financial factors; other factors, such as their ability to constantly supply products or services, flexibility to allow changes, and delivery times, are not considered. The main issue that I have noticed with expansion projects is that most vendors are able to completely satisfy the items on the technical compliance list. Therefore, they all obtain the same scores for technical evaluation. The only criterion left for the evaluation of the vendors is the financial offer. In other words, the vendor who offers the cheapest price will be selected.

9.4 Solutions and Recommendations

Supplier selection is one of the critical processes related to competitive advantage. It has a direct influence on the success of the project; however, it is one of the most complex areas to handle. The telecommunications industry requires long-term investment; therefore, vendor selection becomes especially critical. Supplier selection is not simple and should be based on a comprehensive approach to satisfy different quality criteria. For example, vendor's past performance record is one of the main criteria that is taken into consideration in vendor-selection process.

Numerous case studies have been conducted on this subject, and most have referred to the majority of the 23 criteria proposed by Dickson (1966). A recent study by Jafar Rezaeia (2016) proposes a three-phase framework for supplier selection, whereby a decision is finalised after vetting is carried out in three phases: pre-selection screening, selection, and aggregation. The criteria proposed in this study for phase 2 (selection) are illustrated in Table 9.1 below.

The first phase proposes focusing entirely on the supplier profile during screening, using a set of non-compensatory criteria (i.e. criteria that cannot be compensated with money). These should include specific questions, such as the number of years in operation or industry-specific requirements, to ensure that the minimum requirements are met. The second

Table 9.1   Criteria (Jafar Rezaeia, 2016)

Criteria	Symbol
Cost of delivery	C_1
Lead time	C_2
Non-competitor on specialties	C_3
Price	C_4
Production facilities and capacity	C_5
Quality	C_6
Compliance on certification	C_7
Sustainability performance	C_8

phase (selection) can focus on compensatory criteria using the best–worst method (BWM). The comparative nature of the BWM ensures that the best alternatives are identified after evaluating the defined rankings based on the selected criteria. The third phase (aggregation) places more emphasis on raw materials, because they have a direct impact on price, which is the de facto standard for final selection. Aggregation is calculated for each supplier, using the final score from the selection phase. It also addresses whether supplier is able to provide multiple materials. Overall, it is a well-rounded method of combining different stages of vendor selection for use in a single framework.

Another interesting study was conducted by Shyura and Shihb (2006), who propose an analytical network process-based hybrid framework that introduces another aspect of the criteria—that is, interdependence. For instance, price might be determined by quality or the relationship with the vendor. The criteria used in this study are outlined below.

This approach proposes the provision of an objective view with the help of the nominated group technique. The above criteria are shared with vendors and the group ensures that there is no prejudice and that all ideas are judged impartially. The process is conducted in two steps. The first step focuses on individual criteria, and the second focuses on interdependence. The final decision is based on relative importance and its associated weight for each vendor. The sample view of interdependence is as follows (Figure 9.1).

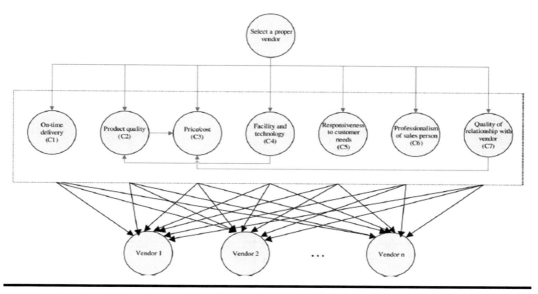

Figure 9.1   Multi-criteria interdependence framework (Shyura and Shihb, 2006).

This method is used to evaluate vendors and hence the criteria are based on assigned weight and interdependence in which the final score is determined. Accordingly, it addresses the competitive suppliers' rankings based on their overall performance with respect to interdependence. After analysing the above case studies and realising the inherent complexity of vendor selection, we propose a simple model. There are only four criteria devised so as to make it easier for Talaseti Telco to make decision based on single-price model. The first three are regular standard criteria that are found in most related search. The aim of the final performance history is to address the reliability angle regarding adherence to the delivery schedule (Figure 9.2).

Description of the criteria:

Criteria	Description
Price/cost	Total price, including final delivery
On-time delivery	Ability to meet delivery schedule
Product quality	Ability to meet quality specifications
Vendor performance	Ability to provide quality support service post delivery

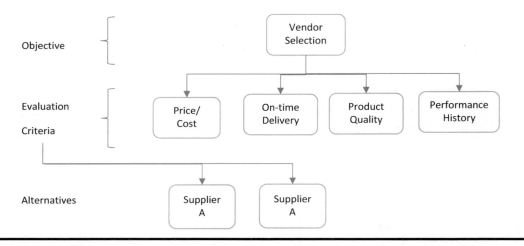

Figure 9.2   Proposed model of vendor selection.

Talaseti Telco follows traditional approach for vendor selection with single criteria of "Price." Any vendor who provides the cheapest proposal is selected. This causes the problem of compromising on quality and vendor's ability to meet timelines and results in delays.

The delays have cascading effect in multiple projects. If one part has not reached on time, then all dependent projects would be delayed. This sometimes enforces Talaseti Telco to alter its product offering timelines to end users. Because an organisation as big as Talaseti Telco depends on its vendors to provide specific products and services to help maintain effective business performance, so they have no way but to look for emergency measure which indirectly increases the cost.

Because of these failures, there have been many improvements to drop poor performing vendors or impose penalties. This, however, does not cover the losses because penalties do not represent opportunity cost and potential profit of new launches.

9.5 Lesson Learned Questions

- Which approach did Talaseti Telco use when selecting their vendor?
- What was the main problem described in this case?
- How was the problem rectified in this case?

References

Dickson, G. W. (1966). An analysis of vendor selection: system and decisions. *Journal of Purchasing, 1,* 5–17.

Jafar Rezaeia, T. N. (2016, Jun 23). A supplier selection life cycle approach integrating traditional and environmental criteria using the best worst method. *Journal of Cleaner Production, 135,* 577–588.

Shyura, H.-J., Shihb, H.-S. (2006). A hybrid MCDM model for strategic vendor selection. *Mathematical and Computer Modelling, 44,* 794–761.

Chapter 10

The Issues and Risks Confronted during an IT Cloud Migration Project

Fayyaz Imtiaz
Ingram Micro

Harish Ramanujam Krishnaswani
Wirecard Processing

Kevin Francis
Kernel Technologies

Contents

10.1 Introduction

Mr Mohamed Sulaiman, the project manager of SplashyU Technologies LLC, had initiated a project for a bank in Yemen. The aim of the project was to migrate the IT infrastructure from the company's premises to the cloud. The main reason for the migration to the cloud was to gain the associated benefits and to enable access to bank information from any location. In addition, the bank had 120 branches in Yemen and wanted to scale its business to other parts of the world. To accomplish this aim, the bank was advised to migrate to the cloud, which would make its IT more agile.

The project, which was titled "Shifting the IT Infrastructure to the Cloud," was divided into three different phases. The first phase of the project involved migrating a critical SQL database (size 1.7TB) to the cloud. The second phase entailed migrating 29 virtual machines (VMs) to the cloud. The third and final phase of the project focused on fine-tuning the bank's infrastructure by showcasing the benefits of the cloud. This third phase was an ongoing activity, which was similar to managed services, in that SplashyU Technologies would be engaging with the client on a weekly basis to determine how best to reduce the bank's overhead IT costs by consolidating the VMs in the cloud. Mr Mohamed will discuss phases 1 and 2 of the project in this case study.

10.2 Organisational Background

SplashyU Technologies is one of the leading providers of expert IT service to both local and international businesses. It is one of Microsoft's Tier 1 Gold Partners in the region and has been one of its preferred partners. SplashyU Technologies has been active in the UAE since 2002, with 2018 marking its 16th successful year in the region. It has a wide range of experience, from implementing VMware to virtualisation in the early 2000s and eventually adapting to the cloud-computing wave as of 2012.

SplashyU Technologies has been identified by many distributors in the world as being the best-managed service provider. SplashyU Technologies' client base

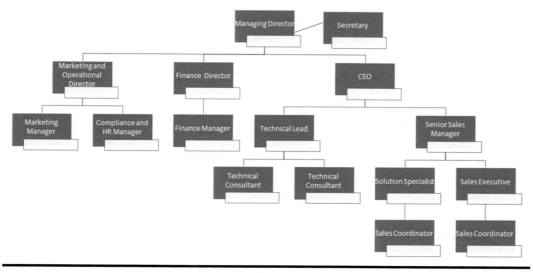

Figure 10.1   Organisational structure of SplashyU technologies.

is growing exponentially, and the company is currently working with a few other top regional companies in industries such as logistics, retail, healthcare, construction, and manufacturing. One of the SplashyU Technologies' main areas of focus is the small–medium business (SMB) market, which is a huge market in the UAE. It provides the SMB market with tailor-made solutions, which can facilitate the digital transformation of business.

Vision: To facilitate clients' digital transformation journey.
Services: SplashyU Technologies has been providing services and solutions in areas such as disaster recovery, data backup, the migration of legacy ERP solutions to the cloud, and cloud productivity (Figure 10.1).

10.3 Case Description

10.3.1 Phase 1: Migration to SQL—Pressure from the Project Sponsor

The high-level study conducted in phase 1 of the project was reviewed by SplashyU's project manager and technical team. The scope and technical architecture for the migration of the SQL database to the cloud was designed by SplashyU's technical manager and technical consultant and was approved by the project manager and project sponsor. However, the low-level design and project charter were not submitted by the project manager to the project sponsor. The project sponsor was eager to begin the project as soon as possible due to certain unexplainable situations in Yemen. The project manager obliged and proceeded with phase 1 of the project by taking a calculated risk based on his expertise. Table 10.1 below showcases the key personnel involved in the project.

Phase 1 of the project was scheduled to be completed within 12 days of the kickoff date. Below is the breakdown structure of the work to be done in phase 1 of the project (Table 10.2).

Table 10.1   Key Project Team Members

Sl. No	Name	Role	Company
1.	Mohammed Al Khaf	Project Sponsor	Yemeni Bank
2.	Kumar C	Technical Manager	Yemeni Bank
3.	Abrahim Salalah	Technical Specialist	Yemeni Bank
4.	Mohamed Sulaiman	Project Manager	SplashyU Technologies
5.	Farhad Bima	Technical Manager	SplashyU Technologies
6.	Mariam Sidek	Project Coordinator	SplashyU Technologies
7.	Sangupta E	Technical Consultant	SplashyU Technologies

Table 10.2   Breakdown Structure of Project Work

Task – Phase 1	Responsible	Start	End	Days	Status
Study Phase	**PM, TM**				
As in study (OS and Infrastructure Software)	TC, TM	1/17	1/17		Not started
Requirement study	TC, TM	1/17	1/17	1	Not started
Risk analysis	TC, TM	1/17	1/17		Not started
Design Phase	**PM, TM**				
Design of management server and other servers	TC, TM	1/18	1/18		Not started
Design of orchestration policy and rules	TC, TM	1/18	1/18	1	Not started
Design of Azure storage and network	TC, TM	1/18	1/18		Not started

(Continued)

Table 10.2 (*Continued*)   Breakdown Structure of Project Work

Task – Phase 1	Responsible	Start	End	Days	Status
Implementation Phase	**PM, TM**				
Azure tenant will be provisioned if required	TC, PC	1/19	1/20		Not started
Azure subscription will be loaded to the tenant	TC, PC	1/19	1/20	2	Not started
Virtual network will be created along with subnets	TC, PC	1/19	1/20		Not started
VPN gateway will be created and configured	TC, PC	1/19	1/20		Not started
DNS will be updated for virtual network	TC, PC	1/21	1/22		Not started
Azure storage account will be provisioned	TC, PC	1/21	1/22	2	Not started
SQL Ent VM will be provisioned	TC, PC	1/21	1/22		Not started
SQL VM will be added to the domain	TC, PC	1/21	1/22		Not started
SQL VM configurations will be modified	TC, PC	1/23	1/24		Not started
Failover cluster role will be installed along with necessary windows features	TC, PC	1/23	1/24	2	Not started
Enhance availability will be enable	TC, PC	1/23	1/24		Not started
New always on availability group will be created	TC, PC	1/25	1/26		Not started
Database will be added to AG	TC, PC	1/25	1/26	2	Not started
Testing the solution	TC, PC	1/25	1/26		Not started
Documentation and Realise – Sign Off	**PM, TM**				
Documentation submission	TM, PC, TC	1/27	1/28	2	Not started
Sign off	PM, TM	1/27	1/28		Not started
End of project		**1/17**	**1/28**	**12**	

10.3.1.1 Impact of Starting the Project without a Proper Plan and Strategy

The above work breakdown structure (WBS) was the first version that was submitted to the project sponsor based on the high-level study done by the SplashyU team. The project kicked off as per the schedule, and up until day 6, the tasks were completed successfully and the schedule performance index for the project was 1. However, on day 7 of the project, the SplashyU technical team noticed a critical problem that had not been identified during the study phase. The team discovered that Yemeni Bank's EMC Networker was incompatible with the SQL VMs on Azure. This was a product limitation of the EMC Networker used by the bank. As a result of this issue, the team was forced to deviate from the WBS and had to invest more business days in identifying the root cause of the product's limitation by working with the EMC team. However, the project had been stalled for more than a week, and the team still had not arrived at a solution. This resulted in a loss of time and money, as well as a considerable amount of effort. The SplashyU team had to rework the technical aspect of the project, considering the limitation of the EMC Networker, and had to device a different approach to phase 1 of the project.

10.3.1.2 A Less Effective Approach

The new approach was less effective than the previous one. However, considering the limitations of the EMC Networker, the SplashyU team had to settle for the less effective design to enable replication of the SQL database to the cloud (Azure). The new approach had an adverse impact on the project sponsor, increased the overall cost of the project, and forced SplashyU Technologies to reduce the hourly rate of the project employees, which was a sacrifice that was made in consideration of customer satisfaction.

10.3.1.3 Completion of Phase 1

After devising the new approach to phase 1 of the project, the replication of the SQL database to the cloud was completed successfully. However, phase 1 took more than 40 days, resulting in losses related to time, cost, and effort. However, because both parties who were involved in the project decided to bear the losses, the overall impact was comparatively less for the project sponsor. The project sponsor decided to go ahead with phase 2 of the project by ignoring the errors committed in phase 1.

10.3.2 *Phase 2: Migration of VMs to the Cloud*

The second phase of the project was to migrate 29 VMs from the premises to the cloud. This was an important phase of the project, as there were many critical applications running on the VMs. The second phase of the project was recently initiated by SplashyU Technologies, and we would like to discuss the recommendations and the best approaches for carrying out phase 2.

10.4 **Solutions and Recommendations**

10.4.1 *Importance of a Project Charter*

A project charter is a formal document that authorises the project manager to begin a project. It includes the project's requirements and scope, business constraints, time stamp (i.e. the expected duration of the entire project), and, most important, return of investment (i.e. the project is profitable upon completion). The project manager, whether independently or with a team member, must draft the project charter. Importantly, the project sponsor has to authorise the project charter (Alex, 2005). The project charter is a key step towards the smooth completion of the project. In other words, it provides the answer to the first question that is asked when undertaking a project: "Are we ready to begin?" Therefore, in the programming phase (phase 1) of this case, the project charter was not drafted in a formal way due to the restricted time frames. All information was communicated verbally, as was the case for all authorisation that was given. Consequently, there was a major lag in the completion of project. The major lesson learned, which occurred after the interview process, was that a project must not be initiated without a project charter, as it is the official authorisation for the project manager to proceed with the project.

10.4.2 *Emphasis on the Scope of the Project*

The scope of the project must be clearly identified before the project charter is signed. Project scope management must consist of the following areas: (1) planning, (2) definition, (3) WBS, (4) verification, and (5) control. Of course, some assumptions will be made and must be considered when defining the scope of the project, but they must not be allowed to impact the project, which is what occurred during phase 1 in this case. Because the definition of the project scope falls within the planning process, we recommend that the organisation consider the planning phase as critical to the project management process. Thus, more time should be invested in the formulation of the scope management plan (Duncan, 1993).

10.4.3 Documentation of the Project

We also realised that no documentation was submitted during phase 1 of the project. This left project team members in the dark, as it is an ad hoc way of executing a project. Most key points were communicated via email and following up and tracking such emails can be hectic and daunting. Thus, documentation during a project is critical, as it helps everyone who is involved in the project to keep track of developments and to go back and review whether any incorrect steps were taken, which can be useful for reference purposes. Documentation can, therefore, be referred to as "progress measurement and reporting," which is a part of the process that comes under "control."

10.4.4 Assessment of Project Risks (Risk Management Planning)

The major factor that makes phase 1 of the project critical is the risk management plan, which, in this case, was not defined. The project manager should always implement a risk management plan, as this will facilitate the execution of the project and enable the team members to mitigate any risks if they occur. The key to executing a risk-free project or at least reducing the risk is to adhere to a risk management plan. The risk management plan involves the processes of (1) identifying, (2) evaluating, (3) handling, and (4) controlling the risks. The project manager should also maintain a risk register to track the risks and issues that are identified during the project (Malarvizhi & Lavanya, 2008).

10.4.5 Coordination and Communication

In phase 1 of the project, situations arose in which not all stakeholders were informed about the status of the project. There were once-a-week calls made by the project manager to update everyone who was involved in the project. However, we recommend the implementation of better coordination and communication processes, as this will keep all the personnel informed about project developments on a day-to-day basis (Table 10.3).

Table 10.3 Project Coordination and Communication

Type of Information	Distribution List/ Participants	Purpose of Communication	Frequency	Method of Transmission
Weekly Status Meeting 1	Project manager, project sponsor, technical specialist, technical consultant, technical manager, project coordinator	• To plan, schedule, and execute the work for the current week. All the work that has been assigned in Meeting 1 must be completed within the next Weekly Status Meeting 1. • Discuss status, issues, and concerns related to the project. Document and monitor key tasks, milestones, assigned resources, and deliverables.	Weekly, Mondays (11 a.m.–12 p.m.)	Online presentation, discussions, meeting
Weekly Status Meeting 2	Project manager, project sponsor, technical specialist, technical consultant, technical manager, project coordinator	• Review the work that has been assigned in Weekly Status Meeting 1, which was held on Monday, and analyse the status of the work—that is, how the work has progressed this week between Monday and Thursday.	Weekly, Thursdays (3:30 p.m.–4:30 p.m.)	Online presentation, discussions, meeting
Daily Meeting and Status Report	Project manager, technical consultant, technical manager, project coordinator	• Report project status; report on project progress, milestones, risks, and issues; communicate risk issues, resource concerns, schedules, deliverables, and milestones.	Daily, at the end of each workday (5 p.m.)	Email (formal written report to all the personnel involved in the project), report to clients and the project manager

If the project manager of SplashyU Technologies had followed the recommendations outlined above, there would have been fewer interruptions and delays in phase 2 of the Yemeni Bank cloud migration project.

10.5 Lesson Learned Questions

- What are the reasons for cloud migration projects to cause cost overruns and being susceptible to delay in completion of the project?
- Why do project managers succumb to the pressure of project sponsors?
- Why do a lot of project managers do not spend more time in the initiation and planning phase of the project?
- Why is there a constant negligence of risk management plan in a project?

References

Alex, S. B. (2005). The charter: selling your project. *PMI® Global Congress 2005—North America, Toronto, Ontario, Canada*. Newton Square: Project Management Institute.

Duncan, W. R. (1993). The process of project management. *Project Management Journal, 24*(3), 5–10.

Malarvizhi, T. & Lavanya, N. (2008). Risk analysis and management: a vital key to effective project management. *PMI® Global Congress 2008—Asia Pacific, Sydney, New South Wales, Australia*. Sydney: Project Management Institute (PMI).

SplashyU Technologies: www.SplashyU.com/about-us.

Chapter 11

The Implementation of Bank Trade Innovation System

Masood Iqbal
University of Wollongong in Dubai

Mohamed Dib
Bank of Sharjah

Jan Michael De Villeres
Dubai Courts

Ali Rezaei
University of Wollongong in Dubai

Contents

11.1 Introduction

"Finally, I received an email from the CIO to initiate the Trade Finance Project," said Youssef, the manager of the IT Department at DT Bank.

Youssef had been working at the bank for more than 15 years. During this time, he had managed numerous projects, some of which had stemmed from a business need and others, which had been mandated by the Central Bank of the UAE. The bank's IT Department consists of the following units: Management, Organisation and Methods, Information Security, Development, Networking, and Support.

Youssef stated to his team members,

> Is it too late for this decision? The current obsolete system should have been replaced a long time ago, when it started hindering the Trade Finance Department's day-to-day business operations. I should call a meeting with the CIO and head of Trade Finance to obtain more information about this project.

He then sent an email in which he called a meeting, and within a few minutes, he received a reply from the head of Trade Finance, "Let's meet this afternoon."

This was followed by a reply from the CIO: "Confirmed."

During the meeting, the head of Trade Finance stated, "The current system is not an up-to-date system. A lot of features are missing. We have a lot of manual activities that have delayed us. I am expecting the delivery to be after the summer break."

Youssef replied, "After summer break!"

The CIO then stated, "We need to have a real-time interface between the new system and our core banking system. This facilitates automatic account opening, posting, and checking financial interest rates using the new system."

Youssef left the meeting with a worried look on his face. Before Youssef left the meeting he said, "Although it is an interesting project, we have limited time and resources to accomplish this task. I don't think we have any option but to start it immediately."

The CIO further added, "The best thing to do now is to send an email to Misys consulting for a solution."

Misys is one of the largest and strongest vendors worldwide in industry-specific software products and solutions; it has over 6,000 employees and customers in over 120 countries. DT Bank's core banking system, called "Bank Master" (BM), was developed by Misys. Consequently, Youssef thought that consulting Misys would facilitate the development of this project. Youssef sent an email to Shaheen—Misys' regional head of services for the Middle East and Africa—in which he outlined all the company's requirements.

11.2 Organisational Background

DT Bank, which was established in 1973, is a leading provider of commercial, retail, and investment banking solutions in the UAE, and it aims to become a major financial institution in the Middle East.

Core Values and Mission Statement: Performance, ethics, transparency, initiative, commitment, and quality.

Our mission is to achieve strong and sustainable performance for our shareholders, and we are committed to accompanying our personnel and clientele alike and helping them to realise their aspirations and objectives. Ethics, transparency, initiative, and quality are imprinted on our methods of doing business and contributing to the betterment of the society and the environment.

DT Bank will be implementing the Misys FB Trade Innovation System in the UAE. The project will be delivered under the Misys "Operating Principles for Projects" methodology. The guiding principle of this approach is to adhere to a standard processes-based application model solution.

The following modules are included as the project scope for the implementation delivery:

- Import and export letters of credit
- Management of shipping guarantees

- Management of guarantees
- Management of collections
- Management of bills financing

The software should interface with BM to automate account opening, posting, limit checking, and the reading of financial interest rates using the new system. The software should also interface with the SWIFT system to route and receive standard SWIFT messages to and from the agreed-upon network (Figure 11.1).

11.3 Case Description

11.3.1 Vendor Selection

Having one bid is worse than having none at all; therefore, proper vendor management is required to ensure that complete requests for proposals are developed and distributed properly to the public and the potential candidate vendors. With the advent of globalisation and the diversity of services that is evident in modern times, it is extremely rare not to have at least two contractors vying for a project, unless the requirements are highly specialised and the criteria are especially stringent. When there is only one vendor on the list, the owners or sponsors should step back and analyse what they are missing and the areas they need to improve upon to encourage at least two bidders, thereby promoting fairness and unbiased selection.

11.3.2 Resource Scheduling

Another issue with this project was that it was being executed during the summer when most staff members were on vacation. This created a gap in terms of both project resource scheduling and execution. Although it was a suitable time to undertake the project because the bank was dealing with fewer daily transactions, resource allocation was limited. With regard to third-party personnel, there was no specified capacity to outsource the project implementation in the contract. The third party was not sufficiently competent in system integration, and an excessive number of issues arose.

ID	WBS	Task Name	Duration	Work	Start	Finish
1	1	**BoS TI (ON39017)**	**283 days**	**602.06 days**	**29-02-2016**	**06-04-2017**
2	1.1	Project Management and Admin	283 days	77.73 days	29-02-2016	06-04-2017
3	1.1.1	Contract Signed	0 days	0 days	29-02-2016	29-02-2016
4	1.1.2	Project Management	226 days	30 days	20-04-2016	09-03-2017
5	1.1.3	Project Documentation	237.88 days	47.73 days	02-05-2016	06-04-2017
6	1.1.3.1	PID	34 days	5 days	04-05-2016	20-06-2016
7	1.1.3.2	PID Signoff	7 days	7 days	21-06-2016	28-06-2016
8	1.1.3.3	Project Risk Register	180 days	10 days	16-06-2016	05-03-2017
9	1.1.3.4	Draft Project Plan	20 days	8 days	02-05-2016	30-05-2016
10	1.1.3.5	Detailed Project Plan	15 days	2 days	30-05-2016	20-06-2016
11	1.1.3.6	Detailed Project Plan-Signoff and Baseline	8 days	10 days	20-06-2016	30-06-2016
12	1.1.3.7	Resource Plan	18 days	3.13 days	23-06-2016	18-07-2016
13	1.1.3.8	Project Closure Report	15 days	2.6 days	19-03-2017	06-04-2017
14	1.2	**Initiate**	**121.13 days**	**78 days**	**26-04-2016**	**18-10-2016**
15	1.2.1	**Project Initiation**	**60.13 days**	**61 days**	**26-04-2016**	**19-07-2016**
19	1.2.2	**Installation**	**17 days**	**17 days**	**22-09-2016**	**18-10-2016**
21	1.3	**Define**	**117 days**	**113.76 days**	**19-06-2016**	**05-12-2016**
40	1.4	**Build**	**135.13 days**	**156 days**	**05-07-2016**	**22-01-2017**
41	1.4.1	**TI Build**	**66 days**	**61 days**	**18-10-2016**	**22-01-2017**
47	1.4.1	**Interfaces Specifications**	**55 days**	**65 days**	**05-07-2016**	**26-09-2016**
48	2.2.11	Interfaces Document Signoff (Trigger)	0 days	0 days	05-07-2016	05-07-2016
49	2.2.11	**Development (Offsite)**	**65 days**	**65 days**	**06-07-2016**	**28-09-2016**
54	1.4.3	Complete pre-UAT testing	10 days	10 days	23-11-2016	08-12-2016
55	1.4.4	**Data Migration Tool**	**20 days**	**20 days**	**23-11-2016**	**22-12-2016**
56	1.4.4.1	Migration tool design, build and testing	20 days	20 days	23-11-2016	22-12-2016
57	1.5	**Test**	**87 days**	**153.1 days**	**13-11-2016**	**15-03-2017**
58	1.5.1	Deploy build with interfaces on test environment	3 days	3 days	08-12-2016	13-12-2016
59	1.5.2	Signoff Installation (SIT Start Trigger)	1 day	1 day	13-12-2016	14-12-2016
60	1.5.3	**SIT**	**22 days**	**65.25 days**	**13-11-2016**	**13-12-2016**
66	1.5.4	**UAT**	**65 days**	**83.85 days**	**14-12-2016**	**15-03-2017**
76	1.6	**Close**	**21 days**	**23.5 days**	**09-03-2017**	**06-04-2017**
78	1.6.2	Live data conversion ready	0 days	0 days	22-03-2017	22-03-2017
79	1.6.3	Go live	1 day	1 day	23-03-2017	23-03-2017
77	1.6.1	Go live preparation	10 days	10 days	09-03-2017	22-03-2017
80	1.6.4	Post Live support (Onsite/Offsite)	10 days	10 days	23-03-2017	06-04-2017
81	1.6.5	Handover to support	10 days	2.5 days	23-03-2017	05-04-2017

Figure 11.1   Gantt chart for the project.

11.3.3 Third-Party Personnel

Vendors or third-party personnel are hired for several reasons, the primary one being that local staff lack the prerequisite expertise and knowledge. There are scenarios in which the vendors themselves are neither confident nor competent, which can arise due to poor vendor management. Therefore, proper background checks should be conducted and stringent criteria established before the approval of any third-party involvement and the finalisation of any agreement is allowed to take place. When vendors are profit-oriented, they tend to manoeuvre around the structures and processes that are in place; this is done for reasons of self-interest and to give themselves an advantage. To avoid or decrease the chances of this happening, stakeholders and sponsors need to be vigilant with regard to ensuring that the scopes and details of the project are clearly defined. Quality should also be considered from the beginning, when the scope and success criteria are being developed.

11.3.4 Going Live During Ramadan

Project managers need to be made aware of the environmental, cultural, and seasonal conditions that may affect the timeline of the project. Knowing the mishaps and gaps at the outset will lessen the impact of delays and overruns. The project manager can offer flexibility by adding more human resources in the form of temporary or outsourced workers to compensate for the shortage of staff, most of whom are on leave. During Ramadan, there must be acceptance and acknowledgement of the fact that progress will be rather slow during this period; therefore, tasks need to be spread out and more buffer days need to be introduced to show respect and consideration for custom and tradition at the project site. Once the fasting period has ended, employees can be asked to do overtime to make up for the lost workdays.

11.3.5 Remote Training

As per bank policy, no remote training connections are allowed, because these can have a negative impact on the progress of the project, especially in situations in which the level of support from the vendor was low during implementation. The policies governing remote training should be reviewed by the project manager in the initial phase and added to the risk register.

11.3.6 Old-Inflexible System

A change in the status quo can result in a great deal of resistance from local employees and management. The project manager needs to consider proper change management, especially if there will be a significant change in the user experience. Knowledge transfer sessions, seminar workshops, and intuitive publications can help in the seamless adoption of any newly introduced automation system. Such drastic changes will not be accepted overnight; therefore, a reasonable period for piloting, user testing and acceptance, and full deployment needs to be planned accordingly. Regarding vendor access, a highly secure environment, such as those of banks and financial institutions, should be underscored early in the project initiation as a part of the constraints and requirements. Consequently, the vendor should be mandated to be on-site and to ensure that the relevant personnel can be flown in to enable them to be present at the premises whenever this is deemed necessary.

11.4 Solutions and Recommendations

11.4.1 Gathering Requirements

It is evident in the introduction, which addresses the initiation of the project—that is, then the CIO contacts the IT manager—that there is uncertainty and ambiguity among the stakeholders regarding their understanding of the project scope and requirements. There is no doubt that accurate information gathering regarding the project requirements is one of the most critical factors affecting a project's successful completion. In this case, the decision-making process seemed rushed, and the stakeholders failed to notice some requirements in the gathering phase, thereby making a change request necessary, which, in turn, increased the cost of the project. One of the reasons for the failure to gather all the necessary information regarding the product requirements was that an insufficient amount of time was devoted to this critical process. The team should iterate the requirements and evaluate and discuss them thoroughly to ensure that they are all covered. More importantly, all the requirements must be understood correctly, first by the stakeholders and then by the project manager and vendor.

11.4.2 Mobilising Resources

It is crucial for the project manager to develop a plan to mobilise and demobilise the organisational and technical resources related to the project. Projects are often delayed or may even fail due to human resource mobilisation issues—for example, if a project team member is on annual leave, but the project manager is not informed of this. Mobilisation is not limited to human resources; rather, it can also be an issue related to the availability/delivery, etc. of equipment (Markgraf, 2018). While developing a resource mobilisation plan, the project manager must, therefore, do the following:

- Identify, assign, and schedule personnel
- Ensure that equipment, financing, and organisation facilities are available
- Determine which specifications and standards are applicable
- Identify constraints and regulatory requirements

After identifying the challenges, our team came up with the following recommendations.

11.4.3 Capturing Lessons Learned

During the project life cycle, many lessons are learned and opportunities for improvement are often discovered. However, the only way to remember to bear the lessons and opportunities in mind during the next project is to review the lessons learned document. This document will help the team to discover its strengths and weaknesses and help minimise the members' chances of repeating the same mistakes.

The lessons learned document is an ongoing product of team effort. The project manager should emphasise its importance, as it will prove to be vital in future projects. It also shows that the team is committed to continuous improvement and adaptive management.

It is debatable whether the project manager should maintain the lessons learned document; however, it is considered more productive if another employee does so, as the document may contain opportunities that were rejected by the project manager.

11.4.4 Realising Opportunity Cost

When undertaking projects and tasks, it is important to conduct cost–benefit analyses to identify potential benefits. One method of evaluating a project or task is to conduct an opportunity cost analysis. Opportunity cost is a major concept in economics that shows the relationship between scarcity and choice (simplilearn.com, 2018). It is simply the loss of the potential revenue from the second-best project.

11.4.5 Setting and Acknowledging Milestones

Milestones are a useful method of measuring the progress of a project, and it gives the client a way to see an important point or stage along the project's timeline and evaluate it before moving onto the next milestone. When a project is being initiated, milestones need to be acknowledged and documented. The client needs to be aware of the deliverables as well as their dates. In this case study, the completion of the milestones is evident. Project requirements could be adequate for the project management team on the vendor's side, because these team members have experience with such projects, but those requirements are not as relevant to the stakeholders as it should be. If there are more specific milestones, the client will be able to detect problems before it is too late and validate them during project's progress. Accordingly, it is a good idea for a client to request a more appropriate or specific project milestone to enable better monitoring and control over the progress of the project.

11.5 Lesson Learned Questions

- What was the main problem in the case?
- What were the changes requested and how did the manager handle it?
- If you were in the shoes of the IT project manager, how would you have handled the change management differently for this project?

References

Markgraf, B. (2018). *How to prepare a project mobilization plan.* [ONLINE] Available at: http://smallbusiness.chron.com/prepare-project-mobilization-plan-80193.html. [Accessed 9 May 2018].

Pitagorsky, G. (2018). *Project management | Managing incompetence.* [ONLINE] Available at: https://www.projecttimes.com/george-pitagorsky/managing-incompetence.html. [Accessed 20 May 2018].

Chapter 12

Health Check of the Business Environment and Technical Infrastructure at Ministry of Society Advancement

Aisha Khalifa Mohamed and Hessa Taha Alhaj Nasser
Ministry of Community of Development

Contents

12.1 Introduction

Mr Warqam Al Asad is a project manager from Levant who has 19 years of work experience in the IT field. He found his first day of work at the Ministry of Society Advancement (MOSA) challenging.

"I need you to head the operation team that will do a comprehensive health check of the business environment and priorities, as well as the technical requirements after gathering the initial information," said Mr Abdulla Nizam, an IT manager at the MOSA, after greeting Warqam and explaining the nature of the work that the latter man would be doing.

After a comprehensive health check that took approximately 3 weeks, an analysis was submitted to Mr Nizam, and it showed several gaps that needed to be addressed.

"Based on the requirements you gave, the first priority is the electronic archiving project," said Mr Nizam after checking the list of requirements provided by Warqam.

To justify the list he provided, Warqam stated,

> As you well know, sir, we work for a social governmental entity, and most of the data on our applicants are sensitive and private. Therefore, we need to make sure that these data are maintained privately and safely in a reliable location. Moreover, the papers in most departments are in chaos and are uncivilised for a well-known governmental entity. We need to organise the historical documents in a place that we can access any time without having them spread everywhere.

"I see. You may start with the project charter till I get the approval from top management. Then you need to start meeting with the business owners to gather information about their requirements," said Mr Nizam.

Warqam was sure that Mr Nizam would require simple, straightforward clarification, as most managers did; therefore, he did not bother to go into the details. The project deliverables and outputs were what the management would ask for.

Before proceeding to the details of the project processes, it must be noted that the MOSA's IT Department has a variety of staff members from different nations. As a result, there are vast differences among them in terms of languages, beliefs, norms, and cultures. In addition, the business owners in the other departments are all Emirati locals, who prefer to have direct contact with other Emirati managers, as opposed to with the staff below them. After sending a meeting request to the team who would work on the project, Warqam was sitting in front of five IT staff from different designations and nationalities.

"I understand that this is the first time you will be working together under my supervision," said Warqam to start the meeting. He continued,

> Teamwork is considered one of the most important criteria for project success. It is the life blood of any project. One hand can never clap! You need to understand that the success of this project will be dependent on all of you, not on only certain individuals. Keep any conflict and tension outside of this building. Here, we belong to the same place and have the same goals. Clashes at work must be dealt with among you. Do not include me in them! I am not trying to be aggressive, but it is important to note these points before starting to work.

Then, Warqam started outlining the project charter and listing the tasks that needed to be done as part of the project initiation phase. Furthermore, he assigned days on the calendar for meeting the stakeholders to enable information gathering regarding their requirements and to design the preliminary scope statement accordingly. Two days later, because Warqam failed to specify who should do what on the project, the team members assigned themselves to the tasks that fell in the areas in which they felt they were strongest.

Subsequently, there were duplicated tasks, because the team did not communicate effectively among themselves, and the result was a massive conflict between the members. At this time, Warqam was heading to the Department of People of Determination (POD) to meet the manager, who was a local female. The aim of the meeting was to establish the measure of performance and gather information from her regarding the requirements for the electronic archiving project.

"Good morning. I'm here to meet Ms Muna. I have a scheduled meeting with her in 2 min," said Warqam to the female secretary at the POD.

"I'm sorry. But Ms Muna has another meeting with the Entity X manager and will be busy with him throughout the remainder of the workday," replied the secretary.

"But I spoke with you, and you said that she didn't have any important meetings today. I also gave you suggestions for alternative meeting days, but you said that today would be suitable," replied Warqam, who was now upset.

"I know," said the POD secretary in a nonchalant manner, "but she informed me all of a sudden that she had a meeting and didn't want anyone to disturb her."

"I see," Warqam stated after saying that he would send another meeting request and hoped that the manager would be free next time.

While heading back to the IT Department, Warqam realised that communicating with the business owners of this entity would not be an easy task for him. He had worked at a multinational company, where meetings with managers ran smoothly most of the time, as the hierarchy tended to be horizontal, compared to the long, vertical hierarchy that was evident in governmental entities. Warqam needed to plan appropriate meeting methods and strategies to prevent the pitfalls that result from a lack of communication. In addition, there needed to be proper solutions to the issue of team conflict, instead of simply delivering a one-time lecture during the first team meeting. Let us now examine how Warqam managed to address the aforementioned issues.

12.2 Organisation MOSA: Federal Entity in the UAE

The MOSA, a federal entity that has its headquarters in Dubai and its social affairs and social development offices across the UAE, focuses on all facets of UAE society. Additionally, the MOSA places emphasis on children's rights, the empowerment of productive families, the integration of the disabled into society, and the development of social security policy. Moreover, it aims to strengthen the stability of the Emirati family, as well as the bonds between the members of society, through its constant innovation, which enables it to provide services in accordance with the highest international standards in quality, efficiency, and transparency.

The MOSA consists of 14 departments that fall under three sectors: social care, social development, and support services. Figure 12.1 shows the MOSA's organisation chart in detail. Furthermore, the MOSA has more than 700 employees—90% of whom are Emirati—throughout its UAE offices.

Vision: To establish a coherent and responsible society that participates in social development.

Mission: To achieve social coherence by developing integrated policies and providing distinguished social services, which are included within the stimulating MOSA work environment.

It is vital to note that the MOSA has three core businesses that provide various services to customers' social security, people of determination, and the marriage fund. The following are some of the services that are offered: the provision of financial assistance to citizens with inadequate income, issuing of cards to people of determination, provision of marriage grants,

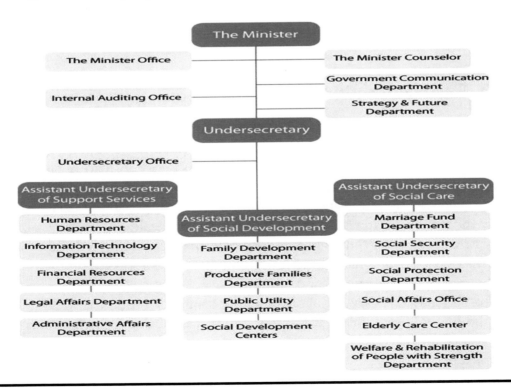

Figure 12.1   MOSA organisational chart.

qualification of newlyweds to marry through engagement in educational programmes (The Edaad Programme), registration of children of people of determination in care and rehabilitation centres, and family counselling advice.

Because the MOSA is responsible for a wide stratum of community members and provides several services that aim to bring happiness and stability to the society, it is vital for it to continue adopting long-term strategic plans derived from the vision of UAE leaders and to introduce new and innovative programmes and initiatives. However, the MOSA is currently viewed as being slightly behind in social services compared to other entities in the UAE.

As previously mentioned, the MOSA's vertical hierarchy—that is, decisions come from the top-down—means that more time is required for a decision to be made and approved. In addition, excessive bureaucracy can be seen in its vertical structures; as individual lines of business become isolated from each other or one department within the organisation is in contact with another, others are unaware of the decisions that are being made and the conversations that are taking place. Therefore, the MOSA was selected as the case study to enable analysis of the challenges that result from a vertical hierarchy—mainly the challenge of teamwork communication—and to propose potential methods of overcoming these challenges.

12.3 Case Description

One of the projects that the MOSA has worked on is the development of an electronic archiving system. This e-archiving platform is called FileNet. Firstly, FileNet archives all documents in one repository instead of storing them in a shared, unsecured network, where it might be altered or deleted. Secondly, it detects duplication; therefore, from the settings, the user can select the option to archive only one copy of a duplicate file. In general, the aim of this project is to maintain private data in a reliable location and organise historical documents in one location that can be accessed at any time by the relevant departments and employees.

The scope of the project involved all departments within the MOSA, and the time allocated for it was 2 months. However, due to communication problems, the project was delayed and took close to 4 months to be completed.

From the above paragraphs, it is evident that two main issues need to be addressed to enable the project to be completed efficiently and effectively.

These two challenges have root causes and lead to sub-issues that also need to be addressed. The first issue is teamwork communication and the second is communication among stakeholders or clients. According to Finch, Hansen, and Alexander (2010), before teaching employees to communicate effectively with each other, it is important for the leader to know how to communicate and engage effectively with the team members.

12.3.1 *Improper Planning*

The conflict between the team members was the result of improper planning regarding tasks allocation. From the beginning, Warqam made an extra effort to explain the project tasks along with the stakeholders' needs, which would determine the budget, time frame, and scope of the project. He also began the meeting well, starting off by briefing the attendees regarding the importance of teamwork. However, he skipped a crucial step in the process: He failed to specify which human resource should be responsible for each task. Doing so would have avoided replication and conflict among the team members. In addition, Warqam should have received approval for the project charter from his manager, in addition of the management board, before starting to call meetings that were aimed at defining the scope.

12.3.2 *Conflicts in the Team*

Although Warqam gave the team an insightful lecture, he made no reference to the personal conflicts that arise when working as a team. He was unable to recognise how the mixture of different cultures and languages could reduce communication, thereby affecting the continuity of the project. According to Thompson (2004), there are three types of conflicts, and it is important to identify their various root causes. The first type—relationship conflict—reflects disagreements that are based on social and cultural issues that are unrelated to work. The second type—task conflict—results from disagreements regarding tasks that have been given. The final type—process conflict—refers to disagreements that result from the inappropriate delegation of duties.

As illustrated in the opening case, Warqam indirectly caused two types of conflicts—relationship and process conflicts. In regard to the former, there was no effort made to strengthen the relationships among the team members. There was no training in dealing with different cultures of team members nor in communication skills. With regard to the process conflicts, Warqam thought that the initial tasks, such as information gathering about suitable software, were not sufficiently important to be delegated among the team members. However, when team members speak different languages; have differing norms, beliefs, and backgrounds; and lack communication skills, the likelihood that they will frequently agree with each other's perspectives is low.

12.3.3 Lack of Management Meetings

Mr Abdulla Nizam gave Warqam the permission to start meeting with the managers to ascertain their requirements, even though he had not had any prior meetings with them to make recommendations for improving the services and seek collaboration within team members.

According to Mr Nizam, "Then you need to start meeting with the business owners to gather information about their requirements."

In addition, because the employees of federal and governmental entities do not collaborate freely in the absence of formal written instructions indicating that approval for coordination has been granted by upper management, Warqam and Mr Nizam should have considered sending such an email or letter to all business owners to avoid the issue of poor collaboration.

12.3.4 Hierarchy Problems

As shown in Figure 12.1, the MOSA has a long vertical hierarchy that makes it rare for communication to take place between individuals at the bottom and top of the hierarchy. As a result, Warqam was unable to make direct contact with Ms Muna, the manager of the POD department, to confirm her availability. In addition, sometimes the middle people, such as the POD secretary, fail to convey the importance of certain messages, thereby resulting in less commitment from the relevant manager. This is evident in the secretary's nonchalant explanation: "But she informed me all of a sudden that she had a meeting and didn't want anyone to disturb her."

12.4 Solutions and Recommendations

Numerous issues have been raised in the previous section. Warqam claimed in the interview that he sat and analysed the root causes of each challenge and came up with a number of solutions to help him proceed more easily with the project processes.

12.4.1 Management Communication

As a corrective action taken to address the lack of communication that occurred between the managers, Mr Nizam, with Warqam's assistance, sent a formal email to all business owners to explain the importance of their collaboration. This enabled him to secure the best deliverables for the archiving projects. In addition, the email included an attachment documenting that project approval had been obtained from the office of the undersecretary.

12.4.2 Team Member Open Meetings

As part of the efforts at relationship strengthening, Warqam held an open meeting during which the staff members were able to freely and informally communicate with each other over food and drinks. In addition, he held focus groups related to the projects, and these provided opportunities for him to become aware of the project members' divergent views and perspectives. This also enabled the members to learn about and benefit from each other's experiences. The outcomes of these meetings were excellent, and during the later project phases, the team collaborated effectively and worked more efficiently compared to the earlier phases.

12.4.3 Segregation of Duties

Warqam settled the conflicts between the project members by assigning different tasks to them, and later, in the execution phase, he prepared an activity list and distributed the tasks evenly among the members. As a consequence, each member was fully aware of his or her responsibilities, thus, no conflicts regarding who was responsible for which task arose among the project stakeholders.

12.4.4 Management Calendar

Warqam overcame the lack of management meetings by conducting meetings based on the managers' availability and time preferences. He attempted to create as comfortable a meeting environment as possible by providing beverages and organising leisure activities for the attendees. Consequently, Warqam was able to meet all managers and solicit their ideas and points of view. In addition, all managers had a clear understanding of the project's scope, requirements, and updates.

After reviewing the challenges faced by the MOSA team during the e-archiving project, as well as the solutions and strategies put forward by the project manager, Warqam, we came up with four recommendations that might help any project manager to overcome challenges related to communication and teamwork.

12.4.5 *Training in Culture Differences and Communication Skills*

As previously mentioned, team conflicts arose due to the members' differences with regard to language, beliefs, and backgrounds. As a result, cross-cultural training should be given to all members involved in a project, especially if they are from different cultures or backgrounds. This training will clarify cultural differences, help members manage these differences, and thereby enhance project's effectiveness (Müller & Turner, 2007).

12.4.6 *The Project Manager as the Problem Solver*

"Clashes at work must be dealt with among you. Do not include me in them!" said Warqam during his opening speech. As per the known norms of project management, the project manager should be responsible for all issues that are raised during the course of the project, including any conflicts between team members. Therefore, when Warqam gave the options to the members regarding conflict resolution, he also gave them the option of not resolving any conflicts at all. His condition was that he was not to be included in the conflicts, and this was all. Hence, we suggest that Warqam should pay more attention to team issues and should be responsible for holding team members accountable when it comes to their work, as well as their personal conflicts.

12.4.7 *Team-Building Exercises*

In any project, once the team members have been identified and the team has been formed, regular exercises should be carried out to help create a cohesive group. Team members need this opportunity to get to know each other and to motivate them to talk and share ideas. By doing so, the barrier between them begins to disintegrate, and the likelihood of dissension is thereby reduced.

12.4.8 The Development of a Communication Plan

Developing a communication plan is a crucial step that needs to be followed during the planning stage of any project. The purpose of the project, the audience, and the communication channels should be identified. By doing so, the individuals who are involved in the project will have a clear idea regarding whom they need to contact and how (Heagney & Lewis, 2016). In addition, an effective communication plan permits project members to remain productive, as they are made aware of project updates. Consequently, they will be more comfortable with their duties.

12.5 Lesson Learned Questions

- Do you think the strategies employed by Mr Waleed, the project manager, to overcome challenges faced were effective? Why?
- How is the teamwork communication problem is affecting the company?

References

Finch, K., Hansen, C. and Alexander, R. (2010). *A Manager's Guide to Communicating with Employees.* Province of Nova Scotia, Canada: Communications Planning Section of Communications Nova Scotia.

Heagney, J. and Lewis, J. (2016). *Fundamentals of Project Management.* New York: Amacom, American Management Association.

Müller, R. and Turner, R. (2007). The influence of project managers on project success criteria and project success by type of project. *European Management Journal,* 25(4), 298–309.

Thompson, L. (2004). *Making the Team.* Upper Saddle River, NJ: Pearson Prentice Hall.

Chapter 13

"Let's Get Our Act Together!" Continuous Improvement between MBI and the Artics

Aoun Lutfi
IBM

Hamda Al Zarooni and Yasmine Al Najar
University of Wollongong in Dubai

Moon Diab
BMW

Contents

13.1 Introduction

Machines Business International (MBI) and the Artics have been preparing and delivering workshops for a couple of years now. The aim of these sessions is to help developers and enthusiasts get acquainted with all kinds of trending technologies such as artificial intelligence (AI), cognitive technology, and Internet of Things (IoT). In this particular project, the aim is to teach people how to build a self-driving car. By using open technology such as Raspberry Pi, and MBI Cloud solutions, they walk the participants through the steps of developing a simple and basic autonomous car.

The team from MBI comprised three Cloud Developer Advocates specialised in AI and IoT. As for the Artics, the team comprised three hardware developers. The aim was that within 1 week, they would develop the hardware and part of the software and then run one workshop on that part. This would include driver behaviour and analytics to understand the car's data. Then during the second week, they would develop the self-driving capabilities and show these in a second workshop.

Building the requirements went fine and designing went well as well. The two teams had a couple of meetings to put the requirements and overall architecture in place. When it was time to actually build the prototype before the demos, nothing was ready on time. The orders were not placed, so that caused a delay on the development of the hardware. In the meantime, the software teams worked in silos and did not actually coordinate with the other teams to understand their current state, so when their part of the project was done, they were unable to test it on the hardware until 1 day before the workshop. Both teams were able to go through the first workshop; however, it could have definitely been done better; the main challenge was that the hardware–software integration was not fully tested, and the teams were not very familiar with each other's work.

After the first workshop, the teams met and reviewed the reasons for why the workshop did not go as well as expected. From the outcome of this meeting, they came up with a set of rules to ensure this does not happen again. The agreement between the project managers from both sides focused on better collaboration between the two teams to ensure everyone is on the same page and putting their best performance.

Surprisingly, attempting to solve the obvious problems shed light on the real gap in one of the teams, which, after the second workshop, became a priority to solve.

13.2 Organisational Background

Machines Business International, or MBI, nicknamed "Big Box," is a multi-national computer technology and IT consulting corporation headquartered in Armonk, New York, USA. The company is one of the few information technology companies with a continuous history dating back to the 19th century. MBI manufactures sells computer hardware and software (with a focus on the latter), and offers infrastructure services, hosting services, and consulting services in areas ranging from mainframe computers to nanotechnology.

With Mr George Romeo being the president, chairman, and CEO of MBI, the company has seen a transformation from a legacy company to a cloud company. This leads to the development of the Cloud, a business unit that focuses on the MBI Cloud services. These are a collection of enterprise-class technologies and services such as software, platform, and infrastructure services, which are developed to help customers assess their cloud readiness, develop adoption strategies, and identify business entry points for a cloud environment.

MBI Cloud helps protect, move, integrate, and unlock intelligence from data whether its possessed data, data outside the firewall, or data that is coming. Bringing together infrastructure and platform services, the MBI Cloud platform offers an assortment of infrastructure, cognitive, software, and services to accelerate the pace of businesses.

MBI Cloud has many products (tools) under a broad portfolio of cloud products. These tools are categorised into computing, network, storage, management, security, data management, IoT, and many more. IoT tool is a service designed to derive value from IoT devices. By connecting your device, the customer can send data to the MBI Cloud, set up and manage their devices, and use APIs to connect apps to their device data. IoT is used in this project to connect the car to the cloud.

13.2.1 MBI Team

Cloud Developer Advocates are developers who focus on the developer ecosystem, from individual developers to education to open source and enterprise developers whose main objective is to help promote MBI and open-source tools to developers. In this project, the main experiences of the team are the IoT and AI.

13.2.2 The Artics

The Artics is a community space working with TECOM. With the support of Dubai Internet City and Qualcomm, the Artics brings stakeholders, including enthusiasts, students, and the general public of smart communities together to foster assimilation of research and leading-edge technology within a Smart Lab located within in five locations. Innovators have access to technology and devices to build software around smart and futuristic services, including the IoT, robotics, and wearable devices. The Artics simply helps people learn new technologies focusing on hardware by running events every week.

13.2.3 The Project

This project was on how to develop an autonomous car using open source technologies and IoT solutions on the cloud. With the Artics's experience in open source hardware and MBI's experience in cloud solutions, the collaboration aims to bring the best of both worlds to the public. The team formed to work on the project is made up of three cloud developers from MBI and three hardware developers from the Artics. Also, one project manager from each side was assigned to the project to make sure their team was on schedule.

13.3 Case Description

The project is part of a workshop that is delivered over two weekends. The main objectives of the project were to teach the public on building an autonomous car by themselves. As the teams neared the deadline of the first weekend, failure loomed on the horizon. There was barely any functioning hardware.

During the first workshop, the teams only managed to show the attendees how to build the car and how to develop the analytics dashboards in the cloud. However, no one was able to actually get a car up and running. After the workshops, the teams met to understand what went wrong and they realised two major areas of deficit. Mr Annas, the project manager for MBI's team, summarised the problems as follows:

13.3.1 Technical Expertise

This problem occurred for a few major reasons, the budgeting, approvals, and the technical difficulties. Delays in approving the budgets resulted in the late delivery of the required main hardware for the project. The other interesting problem was technical, and this, we discovered during the second phase; the hardware was simply incomplete because the developers could not complete it.

"This was a new thing to me, and I have never actually heard of a case where a project failed because the developers were not able to complete it. They simply did not know and could not, or did not do sufficient effort, to find out how to," expressed by Mr Annas.

These problems revolved around getting the actual car up and running. In this case, the team got their software ready on time; however, there was no hardware to test on. This gave rise to the challenge of actually verifying the functionality of the software.

13.3.2 Time

"The main problem we could denote was having the hardware ready right on time for us to test our software on," said Mr Annas.

"The real challenge resulted from not having the main parts delivered on time so that the hardware developers were not able to actually connect everything together correctly and on time. We arrived at the workshop with a barely functioning car, even though all the cloud components were up and ready," added Mr Annas.

The delay in delivering the required hardware was an indirect cause of some of the technical challenges. If the parts had arrived on time, it may have been possible for the hardware team to actually manage to do something or replace some of the members.

13.3.3 Communication

Moreover, a misunderstanding happened between the two teams regarding the full functionality of the car. This is primarily because each team worked in a silo, and none was well aware of what was happening with the other. This problem worsened the situation, causing the software team to only realise the problems with the hardware very late in the project phase.

After the review meeting at the end of the first workshop, both teams met on Tuesday morning and agreed to build the second phase on a certain type of hardware and run a piece of code on the hardware that can capture sensor data and a camera feed.

"By the end of the day, a misunderstanding occurred where the hardware team assumed that the image processing will be done on the hardware, which is technically not possible. Only the image capture will run on the hardware," said Mr Annas.

Such a misunderstanding caused a delay in the duration of the project that could have been used to make a better working piece of hardware. After identifying these problems that occurred in the execution of phase one, the teams decided on a solution for the second phase.

13.4 Solutions and Recommendations

After the end of the first workshop, an attempt at solution seeking was undertaken. The two teams of the joint project met and decided that at this stage, some serious action was necessary.

To begin with, the hardware and software teams decided that they should no longer be located remotely and that rather they should collocate and add value to the project from the same working space. They wanted to address the issue of communication and found it handier to be placed together to familiarise themselves with each other and how far each has gotten on their part of the project execution.

They also agreed on allocating a single, fully dedicated project manager to both teams as a single whole. This would put one person in responsibility and accountability for the entire project and give him the time that he needs to ensure smooth and correct workflow. That is when Mr Annas was assigned as a dedicated project manager.

Moreover, the team has decided that starting from the second week, the project had to run in an agile manner. Agile methodology is a project management process in which a team can manage a project by breaking it up into several stages and involving constant collaboration with stakeholders and continuous improvement and iteration at every stage (Wrike Inc., 2019). The agile methodology uses short development cycles called sprints to focus on continuous improvement in the development of a product or service (Alexander, 2018).

As such, the team wanted to run brief meetings to keep each other updated at all times much more frequently. They wanted to do this at the end of every sub-scope. They did this and cut their big scope into five smaller scopes, two relating to hardware and three to software. With the agile methodology, Mr Annas was able to efficiently manage the time and efforts of those involved, and actually, find the root cause of the problems. Even despite all this, there still remains one major challenge: At the end of the project, the hardware scopes were still left unmet. Root cause analysis and agile techniques helped identify that the main problem is in the skill set available, not with anything else.

The project failed to deliver on scope within the fixed time and budget. After attempting to solve the problem through a dedicated project manager and applying the agile methodology and through collocating the teams to the same working space, and towards the end of the project's dedicated time, the real problem showed up. The hardware team had technical deficiencies. The team members may need to be replaced or trained for future purposes. Nonetheless, the second workshop was delivered successfully given the status of the project.

A change in the management style in the project helped uncover the problem; the main issue with the project is that there should have been a dedicated project manager to be able to properly monitor and control the situation when the first signs of the problem showed up. Even though the project was not 100% successful, this does not mean that the management style chosen was bad, or it does not mean that the actions taken were wrong. This means that if both teams have not acted and learned from the first phase of the project, things could have been worse. The change the teams have undergone was managed properly, which is reflected in the fact that the main problem was actually contained to some extent.

Agile also relatively mitigated the results; with the continuous improvement and learning values inherent in agile, this forced the teams to find a solution. Also, since agile focuses on delivering small functional parts at small time intervals, this ensured that the teams have at least part of the scope ready for delivery during the workshop (Project Management Institute, 2017).

Even though the solution implemented helped mitigate the failure, the teams could have implemented other solutions to make things better. Once the teams realised the real cause of the failure, they could have sourced another hardware developer to fill the skills gap. Since the teams realised the gap, there was a couple of days remaining for the workshop, during these 2 days, this sourced developer could probably have completed one other scope.

Another alternative could have been to postpone the workshop day. Since little to no additional cost would be involved with rescheduling, it might have been reasonable to postpone and work on delivering the full package. However, one key feature of agile is that it does not promise the delivery of a fully working product by the end of a time period; however, it aims to deliver as many functional portions as possible in each sprint or phase. This may justify not rescheduling; however, it may not be the case in this project.

Even though the teams failed to deliver the project scope fully, they managed to deliver part of a project and uncover a skill gap in hardware development. After all, the aim of agile is continuous improvement, which definitely ended up in a very valuable lesson for both teams. The actions taken after the first iteration managed to salvage parts of the project and deliver part of it; nonetheless, more could have been done to avoid the situation. A choice between the delay of project submission or submission of an incomplete project was the main dilemma. Despite the teams' choice of submitting on time, they could have done better by recruiting more skills to compensate for the gap realised during the second phase.

Both teams decided to host the third workshop 3 weeks after the second workshop to complete the missing components. With the lessons learned, they aimed to complete everything in time and on the scope this time.

13.5 Lesson Learned Questions

■ What were the causes of the issues highlighted in the case study?
■ What are the roles of the project manager in this case?
■ What were the steps taken to rectify the issues?

References

Alexander, M. (2018). Agile project management: A comprehensive guide. CIO. [ONLINE]. Available at: www.cio.com/article/3156998/agile-project-management-a-beginners-guide.html [Accessed 15 December 2018].

Project Management Institute. (2017). *Agile Practice Guide*. Newtown Square, PA: Project Management Institute.

Wrike Inc. (2019). Project management guide FAQ. [ONLINE]. Available at: www.wrike.com/project-management-guide/faq/what-is-agile-methodology-in-project-management/. [Accessed 3 January 2019].

Index